THE YEAR
I WAS
TERMINAL

KATHY HEEB

Some of the names and locations in this book have been changed to protect the privacy of the individuals. The author of this book does not dispense medical advice, nor prescribe the use of any treatment or nutritional formulations as a form of treatment for any medical problems without the advice of a licensed physician or therapist. The book contains general information and is not intended to be, nor should be, used as a substitution for specific medical advice.

Taffy Dawn Books

A Division of Kathy B Corp

1325 Boland Pl

St. Louis, MO 63117

For information about special discounts for bulk purchases, please contact Kath B Corp Special Sales at 314-266-9827 or ch@stlcatholicmedia.com

Jacket design by **Chris Heeb**

Manufactured in the United States of America

Library of Congress Cataloging-in-Publication Data

ISBN. **979-8-9903493-0-8**

TABLE OF CONTENT

Foreword

As winter draws to a close and glimpses of spring emerge in St. Louis, Missouri, I find myself overwhelmed with profound gratitude and awe. The journey chronicled within these pages is not merely a tale of love and resilience; it is a testament to the miraculous power of faith, prayer, and the indomitable human spirit.

What began as stage 2 breast cancer and later progressed to stage 4 has been a trial by fire for my wife, a journey fraught with uncertainty, fear, and unimaginable challenges. From the moment of her diagnosis, our lives were forever altered, and yet, amidst the darkness, she found a light that refused to be extinguished.

The beauty of this story lies in its compelling exploration into the depths of one's being. It has evolved into a narrative that will touch thousands, if not hundreds of thousands of people throughout the world.

In the face of daunting odds and a prognosis that offered little hope, my wife chose to fight with every fiber of her being. With unwavering faith as her shield and prayer as her anchor, she embarked on a healing journey that defied medical expectations and surpassed all human understanding. Kathy clung to her faith like a lifeline, defying the odds and leaving doctors scratching their heads in disbelief.

Through the grace of God and the dedication of a biochemist and her innovative mushroom concentrate drink, my wife embraced an experimental "all-natural" treatment that offered a glimmer of hope where none seemed to exist. Day by day, step by step, she forged ahead with courage and determination, facing the uncertainties and challenges of her journey head-on. Together, we acknowledged the experimental nature of the treatment, understanding that its effectiveness was uncertain. Despite the odds, she bravely rewrote the narrative of her own survival.

Yet, her journey was not solely one of physical healing; it was a journey of the soul, a testament to the power of love, faith, and the enduring resilience of the human spirit. In the darkest of moments, she clung to her faith like a lifeline, drawing strength from the promise of a higher power and the unwavering support of loved ones by her side.

At times, the weight of helplessness bore down on me like a relentless storm, watching my wife endure pain and uncertainty. I grappled with anger and frustration, questioning why she had to endure such a cruel fate. It felt like I was drowning in a sea of despair, clutching at straws for any semblance of hope. In those moments of darkness, she remained my unwavering beacon of strength, her resilience a testament to the human spirit's capacity to endure. Despite my struggles, her unwavering determination and faith inspired me to soldier on. She became my rock, reassuring me that even amidst the darkest of nights, there would eventually be dawn.

As I look back on this difficult time, I am reminded of the countless prayers whispered in the silence of the night, the tears shed in moments of despair, and the unshakeable belief that guided us through the storm. I see echoes of our shared struggles, our moments of triumph, and the profound grace that carried us through it all. And it continues today with a clearer understanding of our purpose on this earth.

To my beloved wife, you are more than a survivor; you are a beacon of hope, a testament to the resilience of the human spirit, and a living example of the power of faith, prayer, and taking risks. Your journey is an inspiration to us all, a reminder that even in our darkest moments, miracles are possible and love conquers all.

To John Lally, Jr., a man I have never met but who made the most important phone call to me at the perfect time—thank you for reminding me of the power of prayer.

And finally, to Alyssa, the biochemist who spent every week interviewing my wife for an observational study. She is more than an expert in her field; she was the earthly guardian angel who arrived at the right time and place, with the right formula, opening our eyes to the power of healing.

Jeremiah 33:6: "Behold, I will bring to it health and healing, and I will heal them and reveal to them abundance of prosperity and security."

Kathy, may this book serve as a testament to your courage, your strength, and your unwavering faith.

And to you, the reader, may it offer hope to those who find themselves in the depths of despair and light the way for those who walk the path of uncertainty after an unexpected cancer diagnosis.

Chris, Kathy's husband

Preface

I keep three books beside my bed: "Mind over Medicine," "Radical Remission," and "After the Diagnosis." The first book advocates discarding the diagnosis and fostering self-healing. The second compiles traits shared by individuals who have overcome terminal illnesses. The third delves into accepting one's diagnosis, embracing life with peace and dignity, and preparing for death. While these perspectives may seem contradictory, I find them complementary. It's a scientific truth that a positive mindset is a potent healing tool, yet it alone may not suffice against threatening conditions. People with sunny dispositions succumb to illness all the time, but isn't life better lived with hope in our hearts, no matter how much time that is, free from the fear of death?

I'm 53 years old and have been diagnosed with leptomeningeal metastatic cancer. This condition, also known as LMD, involves cancer cells infiltrating the cerebrospinal fluid, a clear liquid vital for brain and spinal cord cushioning, and the leptomeninges, the protective membranes encasing the brain and spinal cord. In my case, my previous breast cancer, which had gone into remission, had spread from my left breast and armpit to these critical areas.

Sadly, there's no cure and conventional therapies only offer a brief extension of life, typically a few months at best. The option presented to me was chemotherapy, focused radiation, and medication, which might marginally prolong my life but also comes with distressing side effects such as hair loss, nausea, and vomiting. Prioritizing quality of life over mere quantity, I chose not to pursue this route.

Although my doctors refrained from specifying an exact timeline, the prognosis remains bleak. Left untreated, the time from diagnosis to death typically spans four to six weeks. With conventional treatment, overall survival extends to approximately two to four months, according to the National Institute of Health. Other Google searches say three months to a year and so I've decided to choose that as my prognosis. It's now been five months.

As I write this, uncertain of its ending, I realize I'm no different from anyone else. Aren't all our lives terminal? Just a month after my diagnosis, my cousin's 60-year-old husband, in great health and a devout Christian, collapsed from a heart attack while driving a go-kart and passed away. His sudden demise reminds us that nobody knows their expiration date. Haven't we all known those who departed too soon, as well as those who defy logic by enduring? It's a paradox I find difficult to reconcile.

In the months following my diagnosis, I didn't expect to feel this way, but for the first time, I'm completely free and at peace. I no longer lie awake worrying about bills or taxes. Not because they don't exist anymore, I just have a clearer perspective these days.

My hope and intent in writing this book and sharing my stories is that somehow you, the reader, can relate to one or more of them, perhaps you recognize yourself in similar circumstances, and maybe what I've learned can also help you heal. God wants you to know it's never too late. It's never too late to find gratitude and purpose in past pains and trials.

If I were to chart the peaks and valleys of my life, it would resemble a heart monitor during cardiac arrest. I've celebrated steep highs and endured deep lows, each teaching me invaluable lessons. I didn't realize it at the time, but with the grace of God, He helped me to learn from the hard and challenging times, appreciate them, and even be grateful for them because I now realize that I have learned so much more during the difficult times than I have during the easy times.

Thank you, God, for the challenges in my life. Though I may not understand them all, grant me the wisdom to learn from them and aid those facing similar struggles.

C.S. Lewis once said, "God whispers to us in our pleasures, speaks in our consciences, but shouts in our pains. It is His megaphone to rouse a deaf world."

I've come to see that every failure, every hardship, has prepared me for this moment. The trials that I thought I was merely surviving was actually God shaping and molding me for what could be the final trial of my life.

CHAPTER 1

Life Isn't Fair

It all began in the spring of 2022, during a hot yoga class. After a decade of devoted practice in the Bikram style, I found myself encountering unfamiliar challenges. Despite my consistent attendance—3 to 4 classes per week—I struggled to maintain certain poses that had once come effortlessly. Gradually, through regular practice, I had transformed from a relatively inflexible individual to a confident yogi, often securing a spot in the front row. The heat of the studio had become integral to my practice, enabling me to stretch further and experience a dual benefit of cardiovascular exercise and strength training. Each session left me drenched in sweat yet invigorated, a sensation I found exhilarating.

However, on this particular day, my balance faltered. Poses I had mastered just days earlier now proved difficult. After class, slipping on my shoes, I lamented to my instructor, "My right foot seemed to have a mind of its own today." I attributed it to my waning consistency in attendance, recognizing that like any exercise regimen, sporadic practice leads to a loss of hard-earned flexibility and strength.

The next class, the same thing but worse. This time it started with the beginning breathing exercise which required us to stand with our feet together, our hands clasped under our chin, and as we raise our elbows, we tilt our heads back. For the first time ever, as I tilted my head back, I lost my balance. I thought, *that was weird. Perhaps I hadn't hydrated enough?* Then I started to notice that I was having difficulty with my right leg during all the poses. As I grappled with my right leg's disobedience, I grew increasingly apprehensive.

The ensuing months were a whirlwind of doctor's appointments and tests. By then, my right foot had begun to exhibit a numbing sensation akin to pins and needles. Concurrently, my balance deteriorated. An MRI of my brain, initially suspected to reveal signs of MS, yielded no abnormalities. Bloodwork and X-rays likewise offered no conclusive answers. Eventually, a decision was made to conduct an MRI of my lower back.

The procedure was conducted in the morning, and that afternoon, I found myself engrossed in work in our living room. It was a Friday in early June 2022, promising a picturesque weekend ahead in St. Louis. Plans for a leisurely drive with my husband, Chris, to the wineries in Augusta, Missouri, lingered in the back of my mind.

When my phone rang, displaying my doctor's office as the caller, a sense of unease washed over me. Typically, results would be accessed through the medical portal. "Hello?" I answered tentatively.

"Is this Kathy?" the doctor's voice resonated through the line.

"Yes."

"Hi Kathy, I wanted to speak with you before the MRI results are available on the patient portal."

A knot formed in my stomach as she elaborated on the findings. Although her explanation delved into medical jargon beyond my comprehension, I gleaned the seriousness of the situation. The involvement of the meninges, the membranes encompassing the brain and spinal cord, signified a grave concern. Urgency underscored her tone as she advised consulting an oncologist without delay. Panic seized me, but I hung up thinking, *okay, it's serious, but I'll do whatever I have to do. I can beat this. I'm okay.* What the doctor hadn't told me was that there was no cure.

As I rose to relay the news to Chris, a wave of despair engulfed me. I had failed at convincing myself that everything would be okay and lacked the ability to hold the tears back. Chris came rushing out of the office and instantly embraced me. "Kath, what is it? What's wrong?"

Somehow, I managed to get the words out, "The cancer is in my spine." And then I buried my head in his chest and sobbed. "Oh, Kath," he said as his voice cracked. Soon, he was sobbing with me as we held on tight to each other, as if the cancer were trying to pry us apart and take me right then and there. When we finally couldn't cry any more, we both vowed that we would do whatever it took to get rid of this cancer.

Immediately, Chris, a retired chiropractor, delved into research on leptomeningeal disease, seeking a glimmer of hope amid the grim prognosis. Meanwhile, I scoured the internet, only to be met with disheartening consensus: no cure, no treatment. The reality seemed surreal. I felt nauseous. *This can't be happening. I feel fine except for my right foot. How could I be dying?*

I checked to see if Chris had found anything that would give us hope. The look on his face told me he hadn't. He looked into my red swollen eyes with his red swollen eyes, tears beginning to reappear as he tried to speak. "This isn't fair. You don't deserve this. You're the love of my life. Why you? Why is God letting this happen?" We had spent our sobs for the day, but the tears rolled down our faces as we just looked at each other. I had no words, but I knew the answer to these questions. Life wasn't fair. I learned that a long time ago.

The Divorce

I was 18 years old, living in a small town on the border of Minnesota and North Dakota called East Grand Forks. My neighborhood epitomized the close-knit community where everyone knew their neighbors, and children were free to play outside until dusk. The houses were modest, lining the streets adorned with tall, mature trees. Residents took pride in maintaining lush green lawns, contributing to the overall charm of the area.

The first 18 years of my life were spent in our middle-class home on that very street. I had memorized every crack in the sidewalk that encircled our block thanks to countless rides on my little red tricycle, Big Wheel, and eventually, my Schwinn bicycle during my younger years.

One memorable incident occurred when I was 8 years old. I excitedly rode my bike to a garage sale, armed with allowance money. I purchased a lemonade pitcher and set of drinking glasses featuring characters from the Archie comic strip, intending to surprise my mom. However, my journey home hit a snag. As I was pedaling home with my newly purchased treasure secured in my white flowered basket of my 1970s Schwinn, I had the thought, *I know these streets so well, I bet I can get home just by looking at the street.* I did well for the first block. What I hadn't considered was a possible parked car, which I promptly ran into, shattering the pitcher and most of the glasses. Despite my embarrassment, my mom cherished the lone surviving glass with Veronica on it, a sentimental keepsake discovered years later while packing up her belongings after her passing.

Fast forward to my senior year of high school. It had been a turbulent year for my mother and me. To be honest, it had been a rough three years, ever since my mother and father got divorced. I was devastated when my father left the house. I adored my father. He was a gentle man who rarely raised his voice. When he did, I paid attention. My parents were both 40 years old when I came along, not planned nor expected. Even though my mom had suspected menopause and not another pregnancy, to my mom's credit, she always said I was a surprise and not an accident. By the time I started forming real memories, dad's comb-over was getting thinner and grayer, but he had blue eyes that would crinkle when he smiled, and his laugh would light up his whole face.

My father possessed a unique knack for making each of his children feel special, rarely addressing us by our given names but rather endearing monikers like "sweetie" or "honey." Because of my brother's mischievousness, Dad dubbed him Charlie Brown. For me, I was Taffy Dawn, taken from the way my brother, 3 years old at the time, pronounced my name.

Dad also delighted in imparting his wisdom and skills, whether teaching me to ride a bike or entrusting me with the wheel of his car at the tender age of 12. In each instance, the memory that lingers is that of my father's confidence in my ability to navigate the vehicle independently, despite my own apprehension. His belief in me left an indelible mark on my self-confidence.

Moreover, he shared his love for activities like pool and bowling, patiently guiding me through the intricacies of each game.

When I was still too young to view over the pool table, Dad equipped me a stool and a shortie pool stick and showed me how to hold the stick between my clumsy little fingers, aim at the cue ball and hit it with the leather tip of the stick. I was

5

about the same age the first time he fit my fingers in a bowling ball and showed me how to stand at the line in front of the pins, hold the ball up to my chest and focus on the arrows as I counted my first step with my right foot, *one*, second step with my left, *two*, third step with my right, *three*, and then my left foot, *four and slide*, as I reached my arm toward the arrow I was aiming for and released the ball.

I liked pool and bowling, but what I cherished most, however, was the undivided attention he lavished upon me. He was a patient teacher and encouraging cheerleader. Simply put, I loved that he loved teaching me.

As I matured, my father remained a steadfast source of guidance and leniency, especially in contrast to my mother's strict demeanor. He often interceded when my mother attempted to reprimand me, and that was one of the things that divided my parents. I was the third teenager that their marriage had to endure, and it was obvious it was taking its toll. I wasn't privy to any fights, but what their marriage lacked was just as blatant. There wasn't conversation, touching, holding hands, appreciation, or kind words. Basically, love.

I was 15 years old when their 36-year marriage came to an end.

It was an overcast and rainy Saturday morning making the day appear darker than the time would suggest and mimicking my sullen mood. I had known ever since the night before when my father told me that he was going to pick me up from my friend's house and take me shopping that something was wrong. Dad didn't shop. When he picked me up, his greeting was obviously forced to sound normal, and then we drove to the mall in silence and parked. I'm not sure why he said we were going shopping. I don't remember going into any stores or purchasing anything. Perhaps my mind was too busy trying to comprehend the bomb that had just been dropped on me.

Dad started out telling me that he and my mother had just grown apart, that there was no other woman, but he hadn't loved my mother for quite a long time and that he had waited for me to get older so that I could handle it. *I'm only* 15, *Dad, I still need you.* Words I thought and didn't have the courage to say. How could I? After all, he suffered for so many years already because of me.

When he brought me home, I noticed that nobody else was there. I went into my room and I sat on my bed as my dad emptied his closet, not sure what I should do. I felt a heaviness in my chest I hadn't experienced before. *This isn't right. I thought he loved me. How can he just leave?* Being the selfish teenager that I was, it didn't occur to me that he was leaving my mom, it felt more personal towards me. My heart was crushed. When he finished packing, he gave me a hug and walked out the door, and from the large picture window, as a fine mist of rain began to fall, I watched him drive away. Somehow I knew that I would never be the same.

When dad moved out of our family home, he took not only all his clothes and belongings, but he took my older brother with him. He took our evening dinners and Saturday afternoon pool matches. He took good-night hugs and "good morning, sweeties". Our house went from warm and full and colorful to cold and empty and gray. Left to navigate the strict confines of my mother's household alone, I yearned for the comforting presence and familial bonds that had defined our home before my father's departure. I thought of asking my brother to stay but quickly concluded it would be in vain. It would be foolish to believe that he would give up the freedom that my father offered. The rationale for me to stay with my mom made sense but it didn't make me feel any better about it.

My parents were on opposite ends of the spectrum when it came to setting and enforcing rules. However, my issue with my mother wasn't solely her restrictiveness; it was her consistent tendency to take everyone's side but mine. Whenever I returned home from school upset due to feeling wronged by someone, she invariably sided with them, often asking, "Well, what did you do to provoke them?" Instead of providing comfort or empathy, I longed for her to commiserate with me, even just once. Eventually, I stopped confiding in her altogether. What was the point, when she would inevitably blame me?

The final blow to our relationship occurred during my junior year of high school at the age of 17. The boyfriend I was dating was getting serious and so I decided to get myself on the pill, "just in case."

One evening I was sitting in my room doing homework and my mother came in and confronted me with an empty pill container she found in my trash can. Instead of a conversation about it, she tossed insinuations around. I finally asked her, "Mom, what are you thinking? That I'm screwing the whole damn city?"

Her stone cold reply, "Well, how do I know?"

Her statement broke my heart. Then it infuriated me. *You're right, Mom. How would you know, because you obviously have no idea who I am.*

By this time, my boyfriend and I had broken up and I maintained my innocence, but I didn't bother correcting her. The damage had been done. What did it matter.

Despite this strain, we managed to navigate through my senior year, albeit barely. My absence from home became increasingly common as I spent more time with friends or working. My friends became my sanctuary, my saving grace.

Before my father's departure, our home was filled with warmth and laughter. However, his absence marked a significant shift. My mother's nightly homemade meals and the laughter that once filled our home became distant memories. After my confrontation with my mother, any attempts on her part to convey love or engage in conversation fell on deaf ears and a cold shoulder. Her efforts were perceived as insincere. I also couldn't shake the feeling of blame she carried for the divorce. In hindsight, I realize my teenage resentment was misguided, yet at the time, I couldn't see beyond my own pain. Perhaps I would have been more empathetic had I felt that she was experiencing an equivalent amount of loss as I was, if she had exhibited any amount of sadness or disappointment, but I saw nothing that would indicate that she was suffering as much as I was.

Except that one time:

It was a Saturday afternoon shortly after Dad left. I was starting to go down the stairs to the basement where our washer and dryer were located. I got about two or three steps down and I suddenly stopped. *Is that crying?* I stood very still and listened. *That's mom. I think she's crying.* I suddenly felt sick. I listened for a few more seconds. *What should I do? Should I go down and comfort her somehow?* The problem was I had no idea what that looked like. I don't know if it was our generation or just my family but we did NOT discuss feelings and we did NOT cry in front of each other.

Maybe she'll be embarrassed if she knows I can hear her. That was just the excuse I was looking for. I very slowly and quietly backed my way up the stairs and went to my room and closed the door. I sat on my bed with my hands folded in my lap. *This doesn't feel right but I have no idea what to do.* And I sat there quietly for who knows how long, my stomach in knots, until I heard my mother come back upstairs. I never said a word. I wish I could say that things were better between us after that, but they weren't.

Financial strain compounded our already strained relationship.

It became apparent that if I wanted a car, I was going to need to get a job after school, and that meant quitting the volleyball team. It was an easy choice for me because nothing was as important as capturing as much freedom as I could. I eventually used the money from my waitressing job to pay for my car, gas, clothes, and spending money.

Cap and Gown

In the spring of 1988, my senior year, I got a notice that the school hadn't received our money for my cap and gown for graduation. My mother hadn't paid yet. I was certain that I had left the order form on the kitchen counter for her. *Maybe she didn't see it?* I put the delinquency notice on the table and went to talk to my mom about it. It was 10:00 in the morning and she was still in bed, which was typical for my mother. She called herself a night owl, preferring late evenings to early mornings. Today, people would suspect depression.

As I opened the door to her bedroom, the blackness was so thick that it only allowed a small stream of light into the room, and it landed right on my mother's sleeping shoulders. Even though the sun was up and shining brightly outside, her bedroom was black as night because of her black-out shades.

I sat on the edge of her bed. "Mom?"

Slightly startled out of her deep sleep, she muttered, "Huh? Oh, Kathy, what is it?"

"I need money for my cap and gown."

There was a long pause. *Had she heard me?* She rolled onto her back. She looked not only tired, but she also appeared defeated. "Can you pay for it?"

"Me? Why do I have to pay for it?"

She heaved a heavy sigh. "Because your dad isn't paying me the child support he owes me." *What? How can that be?* This was the first time I had heard my mom say anything derogatory about my dad, let alone anything about money. It was a sad, sincere statement. *Would Dad really do that to me?* It stabbed me in the heart and made me feel like he didn't care about me anymore.

I could feel the tears beginning to form in my eyes. Other kids were getting new cars for graduation, I couldn't even get my cap and gown paid for. With my head bowed, looking at my hands, I said quietly so that my mom wouldn't hear my voice break, "It's not fair."

My mother paused, and in a very delicate tone, she said, "Honey, life isn't fair." And it wasn't a flippant remark, it wasn't mean. It was the tone you use when you're telling someone something that, once spoken, can never be taken back and will forever impact the person receiving the information, such as a death of someone close to them. I didn't realize it at the time, but that would be the most impactful thing my mother ever told me. Learning that life wasn't fair, from that moment on, kept me from ever feeling like a victim.

It didn't dawn on me until I was much older, after she had passed, that when mom told me life wasn't fair, she was speaking from experience. I mean, is there anything more unfair than losing a child to cancer or disease?

Bradley

There was a family photo that hung in my parents' bedroom from the time of my first memories until we packed up the house to get it ready for sale after my mom passed. It was a family that I didn't know. It depicted much younger versions of my mother and father, a small girl that resembled my sister, and then a slightly older boy whom I didn't know at all. I knew his

11

name was Brad, however. At least that's what I had been told from the time I can remember. The narrative I learned from a young age was that was my brother Brad who died when he was 7 from a brain tumor. I could recite it without a thought and without a feeling. Growing up, nothing else was ever said about it. They never mentioned Brad and I never asked. Again, it wasn't until much later that I learned more about Brad.

My parents married at the tender ages of 17 and 18, but they were in their mid 20s when they had their first child, Brad. Everyone was so excited for my parents and everyone loved Brad. He was a beautiful little blond-haired, blue-eyed angel. He had a sweet thoughtful demeanor even as a young baby. When he was 2 years old my mother noticed that something was wrong with his balance and she took him to the doctors immediately. After many tests it was determined he had a brain tumor. Thankfully, they were able to remove it but the doctors recommended to my mom and dad that they think about having another child. They were told that they were uncertain of Brad's long-term prognosis.

With my brother's precarious future, my mother was hesitant to take on the task of having another child, but my father was persistent and so she consented. When Brad was 4 years old, my sister Sherry came along, mimicking the same blond hair and blue eyes. Brad was thrilled to have a little sister and showered her with love and kindness.

Sadly, within just a few years, the cancer returned in his spine. There was no cure and no treatment. As the cancer made its way up my brother's spine, it slowly paralyzed him, starting with his feet and legs. I can see in my head the old black and white photos of a beautiful blond little boy with a crew cut and sparkling eyes, squinting at the sun but smiling a big cheerful smile from a wheelchair, my sister standing proudly next to him in her little dress with puffy shoulders and Mary Jane shoes.

Eventually Brad was confined to a hospital bed that had been brought into our home and placed in our living room. My mother was vigilantly by his side, literally emptying his bowels for him since he had lost bowel function, making sure he was clean and comfortable. Through God's mercy he was not in pain.

One day, Brad asked my mom, "Mom, am I going to die?"

When I think of that moment, I wonder what I would have said to my dying son. I'm not sure I could have been as eloquent in my response as my mother was. I can hear her reply being as sincere and loving as when she told me life wasn't fair, "Oh, honey, everybody dies."

After Bradley passed away, he was buried at Rest Haven Cemetery that was a few miles outside of town. It was a quiet cemetery with very few occupied plots. However, the seven acres were very tranquil and serene, with sprawling green grass and crab apple trees along the perimeter. Within a few years of Brad's passing, when the owners of the cemetery began neglecting their duty to maintain it, they handed the cemetery over to my parents in lieu of court action.

From that point onward, summer weekends were dedicated to tending to the cemetery alongside my father mowing grass and my mother planting flowers. As a child, the cemetery became my playground, where I spent summers running around, climbing trees, conversing with the towering statue of Jesus at its center, and indulging in the tiny crab apples until I achieved a good and proper bellyache. At the age of 12, I learned to operate the riding lawn mower, joining in the perpetual summer task of maintaining the seven-acre property.

Soon after my father assumed ownership of the cemetery, he decided to allocate a portion of it for pets. Over the years, we laid to rest dogs, cats, gerbils, guinea pigs, and even a horse, with some families purchasing matching plots for their beloved pets to rest side by side.

One chilly, rain-soaked spring day when I was 10, I returned home from school to find a basket in our screened-in porch covered with a blanket. Curiosity piqued, I lifted the covering to reveal a small deceased dog, wet and soiled. Though not startled, I was struck by the sight. My father explained that the dog belonged to a little girl who wished to bid farewell before burial so her father wanted to wash and groom the dog so it would appear presentable. This poignant memory underscored a father's love for his daughter, leaving an indelible mark on my heart.

When my father lost his home in the devastating flood of 1997, he moved to the place where he had always felt peace and tranquility. He set a modular house on a corner of the property at the cemetery. When declining health prohibited him from mowing, he would sit for hours at his kitchen table, gazing out of the large picture window. After his death, the house and cemetery were passed on to my brother who now enjoys the same solitude with his family. My brother is now the keeper of not only my brother's resting spot, but my parents' and both of my grandmothers'.

Today, a monument stands in honor of my father, acknowledging his unwavering dedication. The modest earnings from the cemetery barely sustained its upkeep, highlighting my father's true motive—a labor of love.

Engraved on the entrance plaque is a touching tribute I wrote upon my father's death:
"T'was for his first born it came to be
That he would come and watch for thee.
And so this place became a haven
For a father's heart that needed savin'.

For 30 years it brought him peace
Mowing grass and raking leaves.
And then one day his work was done,
And so he went to join his son."

Accompanying the inscription is a black and white photograph of my father and Bradley, hand in hand, walking towards the camera with a serene lake in the background, the sun shining on their smiling faces.

During my mother's final days in the hospital, my sister sat by her side. Despite being on morphine, my mother remained lucid. At one point, she told my sister, "Sherry, Riley is calling for you." Riley was my sister's blond-haired, blue-eyed, 7-year-old son. Assuming it was a result of the medication, my sister dismissed it, unaware of the profound significance. A few days later, as I lay beside my mother, she glanced out the window towards the hospital roof and asked, "Kathy, what are all those people doing out there?" My sister, seated nearby, glanced out but saw only the roof. Assuming my mother was hallucinating, she exchanged a sympathetic look with me. However, from my position beside my mother, I saw what she saw—the reflection of the nurses' station across the hall. She may have been confused by what she was seeing, but she was seeing it nonetheless.

I firmly believe that the voice my mother heard, that of a small boy calling out for his mom, belonged to Brad, not Riley. And when my mom finally passed over, I found solace in imagining them running to each other with arms outstretched —a moment of pure, unadulterated joy. And some day, perhaps soon, I look forward to the same reunion.

God, life can be unbearably unfair at times and we struggle to feel your presence and love for us. In such moments, help us to remember You are still good and Your mercy is available to those who seek it.

CHAPTER 2

Don't Give Up

It's been six months since my diagnosis and I now walk with the aid of a walker called a Rollator. It's a walker with wheels, brakes, and also a seat I can rest on if my legs get too tired. Occasionally I dream at night that I am walking and skipping and jogging and I am so happy and joyful. I am saying to whoever happens to be with me in that particular dream, "Look at me! I'm walking all by myself with no walker!" It feels amazing. I feel so light! So free! And then I wake up.

Before I even open my eyes, I take stock of what my body is feeling like at that moment. Sometimes, right at that moment, I might be so comfortable that I don't feel anything. Those are my favorite moments. I relish that moment like a hot mug of steaming coffee on a cold, wintery day. I will picture in my mind throwing the covers back and bouncing out of bed like I used to, without a thought.

I often envision myself practicing the hot yoga routines I once relished. Standing in a heated room, sweat dripping, balancing on one leg, the other extended at a 90-degree angle, hands clasped beneath my foot. I can almost feel the stretch of my outstretched leg, the strength of the leg I am balancing on. The memory floods me with a sense of achievement, recalling the gradual progress from initial wobbling to mastering each pose through dedicated effort and concentration. Each pose was difficult and required immense concentration, but I loved it.

As consciousness gradually takes hold, I become aware of the heaviness in my legs, particularly pronounced in the mornings and nights. They feel burdened, as if filled with cement, yet not entirely devoid of sensation. Despite their weight, I can still perceive touch upon my skin.

Turning my attention to my elbows, I note a newfound soreness that I would expect after doing an army crawl on hard flooring. While mostly tolerable during the day, it becomes a minor annoyance at night, especially when rolling over in bed, a task that now requires concerted effort and deep breaths to navigate.

Moving to my fingers, I'm greeted by a recurring sensation of swelling and soreness, particularly in my right hand. Before I look, I expect my hand to be as large as a catcher's mitt, and every morning I am happy to find that it looks normal. Although they've been numb for weeks, I instinctively press each fingertip against my thumb, a ritualistic reassurance of their unchanged state. I once again wonder how much longer I will be able to work as a court reporter, and then I remind myself that I've been thinking that since I was diagnosed, and even more so after my hands and fingers started going numb, but each day that I am assigned to work, I sit down at my stenograph machine and let my brain and fingers do the dance that they have been taught and have done effortlessly for the past 30 years.

Shifting onto my back, I observe the sensations in my abdomen and torso, varying in intensity from day to day. I often have a slight pain or discomfort on the right side of my abdomen. It does not feel muscular, nor like a particular organ is in distress. It's similar to a side ache you would get if you were running too soon after eating. It's another regular part of my existence now and so I do not concern myself with it.

Occasionally, sensations manifest in my head, their intensity and location unpredictable. And they are just that, sensations. They're not painful, it's not exactly a headache, and they are somewhat brief. Sometimes I wonder what is causing those sensations. *Is the cancer further up my spine? Is it nearing my brain?* I quickly push the thought away. I tuck it away and save that worry for another day, for a day I don't let myself think about.

So many things run through my mind before I even get out of bed. What will this day have in store for me? I will say a prayer to Jesus, *please give me the strength I need today. Please just be with me.* I count the months since I was diagnosed. I congratulate myself for doing as well as I am. If I think about the day ahead of me too much, it is harder to get out of bed. Often, just thinking about the act of getting out of bed can exhaust me and delay my departure by at least 20 minutes. I wonder, when will my strength end? Every day it gets harder, and just when I think it can't be harder than this, the next day or week it gets harder. That's when I have to really dig in, trust God, and stop myself from thinking about what happens next, when I may be unable to walk.

And then I remind myself, this is temporary. My present situation is not permanent. At some point in my not-too-distant future my circumstances are going to change. I will either be healed or I will go to Heaven. Right now I have to put my head down and push against the storm, step by step. No looking back and no looking forward. Just set myself on the right path and plow through it and I will eventually be out of it, my scenery will change, and I will enjoy the sun again. And I know this for a fact because God told me that Himself.

19

The Eyes of God

Mount Vernon, New York; July 1994: I could feel the sweat dripping down my back as I awaited the 1:19 p.m. Metro North train to Grand Central Station in Manhattan. With court reporting school from 8:00 a.m. to 1:00 p.m. every day, followed by work in the city from 2:00 to 10:00 p.m., my schedule left little room for respite. I might have lingered in my car a few more minutes to evade the heat, but the air conditioning was out in my aging Buick Century. I had hoped to find relief from the stifling humidity on the train platform, but no such luck awaited me there. The longer I stood there, any patience I had had up to that moment was being engulfed by the humidity. It had only been a few minutes but I could already feel my clothes starting to stick to my skin. As I stood there steaming, literally and figuratively, all I could think of was how tired I was and how hard it had been to breathe lately. I felt like my whole body was under water, and giant weights were resting on my shoulders so that just my face was peeking through the top of the water. The water was right up to my nose and mouth, and if one more ounce was added to those weights, I would go under. The humidity just intensified the struggle, like someone then put a wet towel on my face. I was exhausted with life at 24 years old.

Meanwhile, back in Minnesota, where I had spent my formative years, most of my peers were concluding their college endeavors, getting married, and even starting families. Truth be told, in the small town I grew up in, if you weren't married by the time you were 25, you were practically a spinster. In another year, I would be able to claim that title. But instead of following my friends to college, my friend Kim and I decided to move to New York to be nannies. Signing a one-year contract, I hugged my parents goodbye and boarded an airplane for the first time in my two decades of life. After the contractual term elapsed, Kim opted to return to Minnesota, while I resolved to remain in New York, spurred in part by a burgeoning romantic relationship, and continued employment with the same family.

The family I chose consisted of Jerry, the father, who practiced psychotherapy, while Ginny, the mother, worked in marketing. When I commenced my tenure with them, their children, Jessica (Jessie) and Evan, were ages 4 and 2 respectively. Evan, a spirited and robust young boy, possessed a tender side beneath his assertive demeanor. Jessie, with her winsome smile, precocious nature, blue eyes, and sprinkling of freckles, quickly endeared herself to me. Often while she was riding shotgun and Evan launched into incomprehensible chatter from the back seat, Jessie would give me a roll of her eyes that would make any teenager proud. As we drove to school or running errands, I would turn up the volume to my cassette of "Super Girls," featuring iconic songs from the 1950s sung by women, and Jessie and I would sing along to "Hey Mr. Postman," "He's So Fine," and Chapel of Love," laughing and acting out the songs.

My tenure with the family endured for over four years, during which time Jessie and Evan evolved into surrogate siblings, and Jerry and Ginny embraced me as their adopted daughter. Though the hours were long - typically from 7 a.m. to 7 p.m. on weekdays, with additional Saturday evening care to facilitate their date nights - the children made the job both effortless and enjoyable.

However, all good things must come to an end. With both children enrolled in school, the necessity for a nanny dissipated. Initially, Jerry and Ginny extended an offer for me to remain until I completed my court reporting program. Yet, within a few months, they expressed a desire to reclaim the modest quarters I occupied. Understanding their rationale, particularly given the uncertain duration, I departed from the family on amicable terms, setting in motion the circumstances that led me to my current predicament.

Thus, as I stood, hot and sweaty, that late July day on the sweltering train platform, I had to stay focused on finishing school, so I could get a better paying job, so I could get my own apartment, so I didn't have to sleep on Sharon's couch. It wasn't that I wasn't grateful for the place to stay, especially since I hadn't had any other options. What made it unbearable was the guilt that my boyfriend's sister handed me with the extra set of sheets.

Among Tim's three sisters, Sharon proved the most challenging for me to forge a connection with. Despite four years of dating Tim, there was an uneasiness when I was around her. As the eldest sibling, Sharon exuded a commanding presence, characterized by fluctuating moods that veered between effusive praise and icy aloofness. Moreover, the dynamic between her and Tim struck me as oddly intimate at times, often leaving me feel like the sister and her the girlfriend.

For the four years that Tim and I dated, I spent most of my free time with him and his family, mostly because I didn't have any family in New York, and my nanny friends still enjoyed spending every weekend at the bars. Tim and I shared a love for the outdoors and sports and so we spent much of our weekends camping in the Catskills, playing tennis, bike-riding, or just about anything outdoors you could think of. When it was just him and I together, he was amazing; sweet, thoughtful, funny. We were best friends.

Regrettably, Sharon disapproved of the extent of our companionship. One Sunday, prior to a family dinner, she admonished me for neglecting to cultivate friendships beyond my relationship with Tim. Fearing her censure and yearning for her acceptance, I acquiesced to her counsel, resolving to broaden my social circle. It was then that I extended an invitation of lunch to a colleague named Christy, whom I had befriended at court reporting school. With her bubbly demeanor and warm disposition, Christy was instantly likeable.

As the day approached, we made plans for Christy to bring sandwiches and we would lounge by the pool at Sharon's condo complex. I felt excited as I thought of how proud Sharon would be of my social expansion. Finally, the evening before our lunch date, I informed Sharon of our plans.

"My friend Christy is coming by tomorrow for lunch. She's going to bring sandwiches and we're going to sit by the pool."

I then waited for her praise like a child presenting their mother with a new fingerpainting. What I received was silence and then finally, "I can't believe what you just said to me. You didn't even ask me."

My stomach jumped to my throat. I felt like my face was on fire. I was completely shocked. I thought for sure she was going to be so pleased with me.

"I'm so sorry," I stammered. I instantly imagined her telling Tim and the rest of the family what a horrible person I was, and tears started to well up in my eyes. I knew I couldn't let her see me cry and so I quickly turned and went to the den where I made up the love seat that folded out into my bed. I got the bed ready as quickly as I could so I could turn off the light and bury my face in my pillow to muffle the sobs. All night long was intermittent sleeping and crying. The next morning, I rose as soon as the sun came up and quietly dressed and left the condo. I wanted to get to Christy's house before she left. I hadn't been able to call her and let her know the change of plans. That was the day that she went from an acquaintance to being a true and cherished friend. She and her husband Mark let me spend the whole day with them. That cemented a friendship that thrives to this day.

At exactly 1:19 the train pulls up to the platform and I am once again amazed and grateful that they can time these trains to the exact minute, because another minute in that suffocating humidity might make me lose my mind or, at the very least, spontaneously combust.

As soon as the train doors open, I feel the coolness lap my face and I can already feel the tension dissipate. I board the train and within just a few seconds I can feel the glistening sweat on my arms and face start to evaporate.

The benefit of taking an afternoon train is that it is not crowded like the earlier trains with morning commuters, oftentimes forcing me to stand. Today I am able to take a seat in the section where four seats face each other, creating more leg room. This allows me to stretch my legs out and get comfortable. I take a deep breath and exhale slowly in an attempt to disengage and shed my irritability.

I start to watch the trees and buildings pass by. I observe as we get closer to the city, it's less trees and more buildings. Inevitably, without even realizing it, my mind begins to wander. I'm no longer seeing trees or buildings pass by. I am staring blankly past the window and at my current predicament. I have somehow managed to wrap my whole world around a boyfriend who vacillates between making me laugh and love him and treating me cruelly and hate him. In the past four years he had become my boyfriend, my best friend, my family, and also my tormentor. Lately, the tormenting had been unbearable. If it weren't for his family, I could probably summon the courage to let him go.

But for the first time in my life, I was part of an intact family, headed by parents that had a deep love and respect for each other. A family that still gathered each Sunday evening for dinner. A family dinner that now included me. My boyfriend, his parents, his three sisters, and myself would begin each meal with the Catholic grace, which I memorized after sharing a few dinners together, and then his father would say a special "P.S." prayer which often included gratefulness for my presence at the table. With our heads still bowed, hands enjoined around the table, Tim would give my hand a loving squeeze and his sisters would slightly raise their heads to share a smile that conveyed their agreement, and I was filled with feelings of belonging that I hadn't had for such a long time.

After dinner, we would all swirl around the tiny kitchen, clearing the table, putting leftovers in containers, and filling the dishwasher. Typically, his mother would be at the sink washing the pots and pans by hand, and I always made sure that I was right next to her, ready to dry them. I loved listening to the banter, the chat, the funny stories, and reveling in how wonderful it felt to be invited to share in this. And it never failed, at least once during the clean-up, the word "baggie" would be mentioned for storage of a leftover, and if I said it, they would all erupt in laughter at my pronunciation of "beggie". That was the one word from which I couldn't shake my Minnesotan accent. In fact, I still say "beggie." And I still to this day smile every time I hear myself say it, remembering this family and how those Sunday dinners saved me.

But my favorite part of the whole day was after dinner, after everything had been cleaned up, the kitchen and dining room lights were turned off, and we would all retire into the living room to watch 60 Minutes. My boyfriend's father had always been an early riser and so he always went to bed early. And so every evening at 9:00 p.m., he would get up from his chair, step over to his wife, and lean over and give her a very tender and sweet kiss. And she would always say, "Good night, Darling." That was the highlight of every Sunday night. That touched my heart in a way I had never felt before. In my house growing up, even when my parents were married, before the divorce, there were no sweet kisses, no good night darlings. There was barely conversation.

So how on earth could I possibly walk away from this family. In essence, if I broke up with my boyfriend, who I did everything with, I literally had nobody. No boyfriend, no friends, and no family, at least within 2,000 miles. And, potentially, nowhere to stay as well. I desperately wanted to stay in New York, but I knew I couldn't do it alone. I felt trapped in a relationship I knew wasn't healthy for me but at the same time unable to walk away from the family I had always longed for.

Before I know it, I have arrived at Grand Central and it is time to put such thoughts away and concentrate on the task at hand, getting to work. I depart from the cool, quiet solitude of the train and step into a hot sea of people making their way to the terminal. I find a gap where I can join the herd and I follow my normal route through the terminal, up the escalators, and into the deli that is located on the upper level of this massive historical train station. I had exactly $3 budgeted for food each day, and so I could get a small container of rice at the deli for $1.50 and then grab some fruit from the fruit vendor that was always outside of Grand Central, directly across from the Helmsley building, where my job was. So just like every day, I pay for my rice, and I head out of the glorious old train station and make a bee line for the fruit cart.

As I step up to the fruit cart, I notice that the usual gentleman who mans the cart isn't there today. At first glance, his replacement looks like a homeless man with some possible mental health issues. I can see that he's not making eye contact with the other patrons that are perusing the fruit. However, I don't think anyone else notices this. After all, this is Manhattan, and New Yorkers are not exactly known for their congeniality. In fact, one of the first things I learned before going into

Manhattan was don't make eye contact. So the patrons simply select their fruit, pay the disheveled man their coinage, and go about their day. And whether it's because I'm now a New Yorker or because I'm pre-occupied with getting to work on time, I was about to do the same, pay my $1.50 and be on my way. I selected my fruit, the largest banana and apple I could find, my typical purchase. I had deemed them to be the most filling fruit and therefore the biggest bang for my buck-fifty.

But little did I know that today would be a day that I would hold and treasure for the rest of my life. Because today, on the hot summer street of Manhattan, the thick, humid air filled with the aromas of roasted nuts, hot dogs, and car exhaust, I looked into the eyes of God.

As I went to hand my remaining $1.50 to the fruit vendor, with his head still down, not even looking at me, he began to gather random fruit from the cart and hand them to me. As my arms began to fill up, I tried to explain to him, "No. No. This is all I need. This is all I can pay for."

And that is when his face lifted and his eyes met mine. Instantly I knew I was looking at my heavenly Father. Our eyes locked for only a few seconds, but time seemed to stop. I couldn't see anything but his eyes and I couldn't hear the traffic or the voices of all the people on the street. His eyes were filled with so much love and compassion, the look of a father to his daughter. Without a single word He told me, "My child, I know you are struggling. I know that life is hard right now. I see you. I am with you and I love you. You will get through this, I promise."

The next thing I knew, I was walking into the Helmsley building with my bag of fruit and $1.50 still in my pocket, feeling a bit in shock and unable to speak or blink. *What just happened? Did anybody else see that? If I told people, would they think I was crazy?*

I don't remember making a conscious decision not to tell anyone, I just didn't. Not a soul. I came to realize that I had no doubt what I had experienced, WHO I had experienced, and I didn't need their validation, nor did I want their skepticism. This was mine and mine alone.

Within just a few months I finished school, got a good-paying job, and moved into my own apartment. Shortly after that, my boyfriend and I broke up. And three years after that, when I got married to a wonderful man in California, my ex-boyfriend's whole family, minus my ex, traveled to California from New York to attend my wedding. Today, his mother and I are closer than ever. She addresses her cards and letters to me as Daughter #4 and she is my Mom #2. Tim's sister Dawn has become an honorary sister to me and his other sister Glenda also remained a dear friend. And today I have my very own sweet kisses and good night darlings.

All these years later, I can't remember exactly what the eyes looked like, but I will never forget how I felt as I gazed into them. I knew at that moment that I wasn't trapped, I wasn't alone. I knew that if I just waited and I didn't give up, my circumstances would change. And I have zero doubt that I will see those eyes again some day and they will say, "My precious Kathy, welcome home."

CHAPTER 3

God Can Do Anything

I've always considered myself an optimistic person, but that optimism was severely tested with a terminal diagnosis. "Dr. Google" says that I'll be dead within this year. But what if I don't listen to them? I mean, whatever is going to happen is going to happen and I accept that, but what about all those stories of people who have survived (what appeared to be) hopeless predicaments? Why couldn't I be one of them? In my experience, no ask is too big for God. You just have to hand the task over to God and stand back. You will be amazed at what He can do.

The Introduction

Yonkers, New York, 1995: I was 25 years old, and I was on top of the world. I was newly single and living in my own studio apartment. I had just purchased my first brand-new car, a Nissan 200SX. I had a grown-up job, and I was making grown-up money. I felt like Mary Tyler Moore in the Mary Tyler Moore Show, a sitcom from the 1970s featuring a single woman in her 30s who relocates to Minneapolis to become an associate producer for a news program. It was groundbreaking at the time for the main character to be not married and not reliant on a man. In the intro of the show, she stands in the middle of the busy wintery street of Minneapolis and twirls around in pure glee, as if to say, "Yes! I've made it!" and throws her hat up in the air. That was me.

After recovering from my previous break-up, I began dating a bit, but it all felt so forced. After several awkward first and second dates, and as I became more involved in church activities, I realized I didn't need or enjoy the preoccupation of beginning a new relationship. I was just going to enjoy life and see where it led me.

I did, however, start to tell God what I was looking for in a man. I began a list: Smart, handsome, kind, funny, likes sports (except basketball – I hated basketball), likes music, AND, I didn't know how God was going to do it, but I didn't want our first meeting or attraction to be based on looks. That had been the case with my previous boyfriend, and so I somehow wanted to avoid the same outcome. I prayed, *God, I don't know how you're going to do that, but you're God and you can do anything.* And then I forgot about it and went about my life.

Three years later I was still enjoying my life in my little Yonkers studio apartment. I was getting more settled into my career and feeling more comfortable with it. I was involved with the church, teaching seventh grade catechism, volunteering my time to work on Emmaus retreats, and continuing to strengthen my relationship with God. I was happy and content with my life.

For those that may not remember or perhaps were not even born yet, 1998 was a very exciting time to be alive. Cell phones had finally become somewhat affordable and this thing called the internet was really starting to take off. Computers were becoming the way of the world. In fact, I had just purchased my very first personal computer, a Dell desktop computer that

I needed for my work as a court reporter. Jessie, the child I had nannied, who was now 13 years old, showed me how to set up an email address and how to get online, but I still hadn't ventured into the wild, wild west of the internet. I had heard that a friend back in Minnesota was meeting men on the internet and going on dates with them. I couldn't believe it! That was crazy to me. She had no idea who these men were. They could be serial killers or rapists for all she knew. I vowed immediately that I would NEVER do such a careless and reckless thing.

It was July, and I was planning to take a road trip from where I lived in Yonkers, New York, back to Minnesota to see my family. This was going to be my first road trip by myself, and I was a little nervous but mostly excited. My sister had helped me plan a scenic route through Niagara Falls, up into Canada, and around the Great Lakes. There was no GPS at that time and so I had a Rand McNally atlas with a highlighted route. I couldn't wait to see my nephews and my niece, my sister's four kids: Riley, 11; Tanner, 9; Taylor 6, and Haley, 4. One of my favorite discoveries about myself is that I absolutely love being an aunt, especially to these four. Each one had captured my heart from day one, and my sister has always been so gracious to share them with me.

I had had my computer for almost a week, but with work and packing and getting ready for the trip, I hadn't really had time to figure out this internet phenomenon. Finally, two nights before I would start my trek halfway across the country, I finished up some last-minute laundry and realized I had an hour I could devote to exploring this new, unfamiliar world. I clicked on the Outlook icon, feeling a curious excitement as I listened to the sound of the computer dialing, and soon I was navigating into a list of chatrooms.

The internet back then was not the internet of today. There was very little content and so "surfing" the internet was not a thing then. There really wasn't much to surf, and so chatrooms were the attraction. They provided real-time online interaction with other people.

The list of chatrooms was long and interesting. You could choose from space enthusiasts to Jewish teens. In my mind, I quickly pictured what each room looked like. There were bar chatrooms, but I immediately conjured up in my mind smoky, dimly lit pubs with shady characters lurking in dark corners, just waiting for their next prey. I kept scrolling. Then I saw a diner chatroom. Having lived in New York now for 8 years, I loved diners. They were comfortable, neutral, safe. And so I entered the room to see what this chatroom was all about.

It wasn't exactly the diner experience I was expecting. It was just a list of comments next to screen names. There were many different conversations happening simultaneously. So much so that it was difficult to follow a single conversation. And it would scroll somewhat quickly as there were many people in the room and so you had to pay attention and keep an eye out for the screen name that you were conversing with.

For some time, I merely sat and "listened," trying to find a conversation I may want to join. Then I saw other people join and introduce themselves, and so I decided to do the same. "Hi. My name is Kathy," I typed. Much like being at a party where you don't know anyone, a few kind people politely greeted me and then returned to their ongoing chats with our fellow "diners." However, one person who greeted me continued to engage in conversation.

The questions started out easy enough, much like a conversation you would have if you were meeting someone at a party. The difference being that when you met someone at a party, you would know right away whether they are male or female, what they look like, a rough estimate of their age. Meeting someone on the internet, you had no idea if they were a 12-year-old girl with braces and pigtails or 60-year-old man sitting in his boxer shorts and eating a tuna sandwich. And, so, many of the beginning questions were getting those incidentals out of the way.

It turned out that I was chatting with a 28-year-old male named Erik. Throughout the next 2 hours as we chatted, I would find out that Erik lived in Palm Springs, California, and he had his own business as a tile-setter. He had married his high school sweetheart just out of high school when she got pregnant, which gave them a beautiful little girl, Tosha, and then 6 years later they had an adorable baby boy, Tyler. He had also joined the Navy for a time but decided to discharge early when his wife had been diagnosed with lupus. And so between her illness, caring for two children, and trying to provide for a family with only a GED, they both realized it was too much for their marriage to handle and decided to end the marriage but keep their friendship intact, and it had worked out well.

I also learned during this conversation that he was roughly 5-foot-7 with brown hair, and he said that he had occasionally been compared to Mel Gibson. I immediately envisioned Riggs in the 1998 movie Lethal Weapon and my interest was piqued.

The first couple of hours was a very slow conversation because of having to wait for the screen names to scroll through until you saw the name you were conversing with, and so at some point we switched over to instant messaging. Which, today, is very much like texting on a computer.

Throughout our conversation, I'm thinking to myself, this guy is in California, all the way on the other side of the country, there is no way I will ever meet him. This allowed me to be very honest and candid during our exchange. I didn't have to pretend anything, what would it matter? We would never meet.

Before I knew it, the hour I had set aside to explore the internet had been exceeded by two hours. At 1:00 in the morning, Erik posed a question that caused a momentary pause in my typing. He asked if he could call me. *Hold on a second here. Do I want to give him my phone number?* It didn't take me all that long to decide that it would be fine. It was just my phone number. Again, I would never meet him. I was enjoying our chat. *Why not.* With my heart beating slightly faster, I typed out my phone number and waited for the phone to ring. *Am I really doing this? I'm sure it's fine. He's in California, what can it hurt.* It occurred to me for a moment that he could be ingenuine, but an inexplicable assurance enveloped me that this was okay.

The phone rang and my heart raced faster. *This is happening.* I picked up the phone. I don't know what I was expecting his voice to sound like, but it wasn't what I heard on the other end of the line. However, it didn't take long and I forgot about that and the voice just became Erik. Over the next three hours, we delved into discussions about our families, our pasts, and our shared laughter echoed through the phone line. Erik's sense of humor endeared him to me and fostered a sense of familiarity as we chatted about music and sports. Without awareness, he was certainly checking off all the boxes on my list that I had given God all those months ago.

At one point while we were chatting, I started to think, *there's got to be something wrong with this guy. What am I missing?* And then it hit me. He hadn't really described his hair. *I bet he's bald.* So I blurted out, "Let me ask you something," and before he could respond, I changed my mind. I said, "Never mind." *If he really is this amazing guy, did it matter if he was bald? Of course not.*

But he was not willing to drop it. He said, "What? Do you want to know if I'm bald?"

I almost dropped the phone. How on earth could he have known what I was going to ask. At least an hour had passed since we had described ourselves. And that's the way the rest of the night went. I can't count how many times I said, "Dude, you are freaking me out."

As the clock struck 3:00 a.m., I reluctantly said goodbye so that I could get at least a few hours of sleep before I had to work the next day. But before we hung up, we made plans to talk again the following evening.

The whole next day this guy named Erik from Palm Springs kept popping into my head. What was going on here? Was I crazy to spend this amount of energy on somebody I would never meet? Probably. But like a piece of leftover birthday cake sitting on your kitchen counter, I knew I probably shouldn't but at the same time I just couldn't help myself. It was just too enjoyable.

The following evening was another marathon chat, but this time it felt like two friends engaged in conversation rather than two strangers. However, with my drive to Minnesota starting the following morning, I needed to restrict the time we spent so that I was well rested. Before we hung up, we agreed the next step should be photographic proof of our appearances. Erik took down my address so that he could send me photos of himself and his kids, as this was way before you could attach photos to emails and instantly share them. Since they were being sent via the US Post Office, aka snail mail, I knew I would be in Minnesota by the time I received them. Erik was just going to have to go on the back burner.

Road Trip to Fate

However, the next day as I loaded up my car and started off on my road trip, I knew in my heart that Erik would not be on the back burner. In fact, we were in almost constant contact my whole drive to Minnesota, thanks to the new handy dandy cell phones we each had. And when we weren't connected by airwaves, he was in my thoughts. *What is going on here? Why can't I get him out of my mind? This is craziness!*

I scoured through all of my memories of our conversations about possible red flags that I could have missed. Coming up empty, I then tried to imagine what he might look like by the description he gave me. The long drive gave me plenty of time to conjure up all sorts of images.

All of this had happened so fast, I hadn't had a chance to tell my closest friend Dawn. However, along my way to Minnesota, my friend Jen, Dawn's cousin, called me.

"Hi, Kathy. How are you?" Jen asked.

"I'm good, Jen!" *Should I say anything?*

"Have you started your trip yet?"

"I'm driving now actually." *What will she think if I tell her?*

"Oh! Well, I just wanted to call and wish you a safe and wonderful trip."

I have to tell her. I couldn't contain my excitement.

I shared with Jen about my first entry in the chatroom, about meeting Erik and all of our chats, how he kept freaking me out by reading my mind. Jen listened patiently and offered concern but not judgement. And then, being the amazing friend she is, she reminded me to seek God and His guidance. I promised I would, and I thanked her for not being critical of me. I knew how crazy it sounded.

Halfway to Minnesota, Erik and I talked by hotel phone where I stopped for the night. I couldn't resist telling him that I was feeling an attraction for him, and Erik admitted to me that he too was beginning to feel something. We both agreed that we needed to meet. The next day, after I arrived in Minnesota, we devised a plan that we would meet in Boulder, a 12-hour drive for each of us, and if we both still felt the same after meeting face to face, that he would return to Minnesota with me for the remainder of my vacation. To my family, this was pure insanity. But to me, it made perfect sense.

Within a few days I once again found myself behind the wheel of my 1997 Nissan 200SX, heading southwest and speeding towards my future. For the next 12 hours I oscillated between apprehension and excitement. The echoes of my family telling me I was crazy ringing in my ears but feeling a deep sense of change and fate in my heart. The closer I got to Boulder, the stronger both feelings seemed to build. About half way into the long drive, I remembered that prayer I prayed a few years prior, "God, I don't want my next relationship to start out being based on looks. I don't know how you're going to do that, but you're God and You can do anything." I couldn't help thinking, *is that what's happening here? What else could it be?*

Within a few miles of the final exit, I pulled over so that I could use a restroom and freshen up after the long drive. I checked my makeup and my hair and looked at myself in the mirror and took a deep breath. *What is happening here? What am I doing? I don't even know what he looks like! What if he's hideous and I'm wasting two days of vacation?* My heart was starting to beat faster with anticipation and trepidation. As I drove the last few miles, my palms were getting sweaty and images of what he might look like bounced around my head. I knew I was on the verge of what could be a defining moment in my life. I could feel it. It was exciting and terrifying at the same time.

We had agreed to meet at a restaurant not far off the highway. I arrived at the restaurant and Erik called to say he would be there in just a minute and so I stood outside and waited. Within just a couple minutes, he was standing in front of me. *Oh, wow, he's kind of short* was my very first thought. Inwardly I scolded myself for not adding tall on my list to God. However, his first words to me in person were, "You're beautiful." A smile spread across my face uncontrollably and in

37

my mind he instantly grew 3 inches taller. I was suddenly also struck by how handsome he was. I could vaguely see the Mel Gibson reference, however I'm not sure I would say when you looked at Erik, you saw Mel Gibson. But Erik was very much the way he described himself, 170 pounds, brown hair, blue eyes, NOT bald. His hair was nicely cut and he had kind eyes. Relief spread over me.

We had an agreement before we met that if we both had the same feelings for each other after meeting in person, that Erik would come back to Minnesota with me for the duration of my vacation. The following morning Erik and I were settled comfortably in my Nissan and cruising north together, laughing and talking the whole way. The more time I spent with him, the more I liked him. He was funny, but he was also smart, engaging, and sweet.

Meeting the Family

Arriving in Minnesota, we were almost constantly surrounded by my family, which can be a little overwhelming, but he took it all in stride. I was relieved to find that he wasn't someone who needed to be by my side the whole time. He was comfortable talking to anyone. He was a contractor by trade and so he could chat with ease with my blue-collar family members. But he also was an avid reader and very much kept up on the politics and news of the day and so he could hold his own in a conversation with any of the intellectuals in the family. Plus, he was charming and willing to pitch in and help wherever needed, and so the women adored him. Everyone spoke accolades of him. Not one person gave a negative opinion of him.

However, there was one point where Erik questioned his choice to join me in Minnesota, he admitted to me later. It was the day that we found ourselves in the shopping mall and we were passing by a pet store.

"Ooh, come on. Let's just check it out," I said as I pulled him into the small store.

Instantly I was attracted to the glass enclosure that held a black puppy that looked like a cross between a Golden Retriever and a Spaniel. He was four months old and he sat so solemnly, watching everyone from his side of the glass, not barking, just observing, a look of longing to be noticed in his sweet dark eyes. The glass he was behind was marked with a price of $100 with a slash mark through it, $75 with a slash mark through it, and then the final offer: $50, includes collar, leash, and water bowl.

"I have to at least hold him," I said, as Erik looked at me wearily. I really had no intention of buying him at that point. I was the first person to admit that I had no business buying a dog at that time in my life.

The pet store attendant went into the back and pulled the black puppy with the floppy ears out of the enclosure and brought him out to me. From the moment he was put into my arms, his joy was uncontainable. He wiggled his whole body and licked my whole face. I finally had to let him down, and he immediately bolted out into the mall. *Oh, no!* But before I could properly panic, he was running right back to me, jumping on my legs to pick him up again.

As I picked him up this time, it was as though he understood he needed to be a little calmer for me to continue holding him. He relaxed in my arms and my heart was doing something I did not want it to do, it started putting crazy thoughts in my head. *I think this dog is supposed to be mine.* I couldn't believe I was even thinking that. I definitely didn't repeat the voice out loud. At first.

As we were standing there with the puppy, a Down syndrome boy approached and wanted to pet the puppy. "Of course," I said, "just be gentle." The darling little boy beamed as he ran his fingers down the puppy's back and over his head. I noticed that he was accidentally poking his fingers near the puppy's eyes, yet the puppy wasn't bothered at all. He just exuded love.

This is my dog. My heart was pounding. *Erik is going to think I'm crazy. Shoot, I think I'm probably crazy. But this feeling...I can't ignore it.*

"Erik, I really think this dog is supposed to be mine."

"Kathy, I have an Akita that does not like other dogs. My dog will eat your dog."

The comment suggesting that this relationship was going to go further didn't at all surprise me. I think by this time we both knew that we were meant to be together.

"No, she won't. They'll figure out how to get along."

I could tell by Erik's face that he was not as convinced.

Maybe I shouldn't do this. It makes no sense. But this feeling...

"I'm sorry, I have to get him. I just feel so strongly that he's supposed to be mine."

Okay, God, I'm trusting you here. This must be you.

Suddenly "15 years" popped into my head. I interpreted it to mean, *Oh, I'm going to have him for 15 years.* When the "15 years" popped into my head, it was like I was receiving an answer to a question I hadn't asked.

30 minutes later Erik and I walked out of that pet store with a brand-new water bowl and the cutest little black puppy on his first leash. I was excited and happy while Erik was wondering what the heck he had gotten himself into.

I tossed around several names for my new friend, but I wanted something personal. Erik and I were staying with my dad while we were in Minnesota, and he was calling me by his nickname for me, Taffy Dawn, which always evoked a feeling of love and belonging in me, and so he became my Taffy.

Taffy was such a well-behaved puppy, you couldn't help but fall in love with him. I could tell that as much as Erik didn't want to form a bond with him, Taffy was able to wiggle his way into his heart too.

After an amazing week together, we both knew we had to decide where this was going. A long distance relationship wasn't feasible. Erik had already told me that there was no way he could leave his children and so if we wanted to continue this, it would require me moving to California. I knew I had strong feelings for him, but that was a big move.

I've had a few defining moments in my life, moments when I knew that the choice I was about to make would greatly change the course of my life. The first one was moving to New York. This was the second one. The third one happens many years after this.

As our vacation came to an end, I drove Erik to the airport so he could fly back to Boulder. On the way, we stopped for lunch. We sat in a booth across from each other. We chatted about nothing, putting off the conversation we both knew we needed to have.

Without realizing what it was, I recognize now that I have always had a very strong intuition and so I was trying my hardest to tap into that as we sat there chatting. As he talked, I tried to pretend I was listening but instead I was playing each scenario in my head, moving to California or staying in New York, and then scanning my gut for a reaction. Each time I came up empty. With either choice I felt neither sick to my stomach nor happy and excited. I still had no idea what I wanted to do, and for some reason I felt like I had to make the decision right then and there. It didn't even occur to me to wait, take some time to think about it. When my intuition failed me, I went back to God. God had placed in my lap exactly what I had asked for. And I mean EXACTLY. I could not overlook that. I decided I had to trust that. I had to trust God.

In August I flew out to California, and I met Erik's ex-wife and his children Tosha and Tyler. Tosha, 10 years old, was a spunky, friendly girl who was all knees and elbows. It was easy to see even at that age that she was a very loving and caring soul with a strong motherly instinct as she displayed with her younger brother. Tyler was 5 years old, and he was an energetic happy little boy who was friendly and warm. They were easy to love from day one.

Another week together confirmed my decision to trust God. I knew without any doubts or hesitation that I was in love with Erik and that God had brought us together. From there, everything just fell into place. My two-year lease on my apartment expired on September 1st and so one week after that, I was living in California, and we were married by the following January.

For 15 years we enjoyed many adventures, laughs, some tears, ups and downs typical of marriage, and I never regretted that choice I made in that restaurant by the airport all those years ago. He had proven himself to be a faithful, devoted husband. He was my best friend and the love of my life up to that point. Every day he made me laugh and feel loved, appreciated, and I felt blessed to be his wife.

I also had the privilege of watching Tosha and Tyler grow up. Tosha went from knees and elbows to a stunning teenager, to the horror of her father. On one particular Friday when Tosha was 13, Erik and I went to pick up her and Tyler for the weekend. Tosha, dressed in her usual jeans and hoodie, pulled me into her bedroom and closed the door. "I have to show you something!" She declared. "I have hips!" She professed as she lifted her hoodie with her left hand and pointed to her hip with the right hand. She was right. She was transforming from a gawky girl into a young woman.

"Don't show your dad!" I begged, and we both laughed.

Of course, it didn't take long before there was no hiding it. By the time she was 15, her braces came off and she transformed into a stunning young woman albeit with the naivete of most 15-year-old girls. She was convinced that the 18-year-old boys that called on her were sincere when they said they just wanted to be her friend. Erik had no problem telling these 18-year-olds when they called that his daughter was only 15 and therefore they need not call back again.

Tyler stole my heart in so many ways. One weekend while he was with us, he was about 7 years old, as I passed by the bathroom one morning, I could hear him in the shower and he was singing. I stopped and put my ear to the door to see if I could recognize the song. I had to stifle a laugh when I heard, "Do a little dance, make a little love, get down tonight, get down tonight." When Tyler was around, the laughs never stopped.

What an honor it was to be a part of their lives. They were unbelievably generous with their love and kindness and I learned so much from them.

When I had prayed for God to find me somebody to love without it being based on looks initially, I really had no idea how that would even be possible. I couldn't conjure up a scenario in my mind at all. But that's what God does. When we hand our desires over to Him and we allow Him to take control, He will surpass our expectations every time. He can turn our impossibilities into reality. We just have to ask Him and then get out of the way.

CHAPTER 4

Thank God For Everything

Suffering requires considerable patience. Any suffering. Whether enduring a temporary inconvenience or facing a prolonged ordeal. Patience is necessary while awaiting a change in circumstances and while coping with the consequences of your suffering. At times, you may have an idea of when your suffering will conclude, such as when you are enduring a visit from your in-laws for a week. However, the most challenging situations arise when the duration of suffering remains uncertain.

In my case, I'm seven months into my diagnosis and so my time could be running out, or not. I mean, God can do anything, right? I could die tomorrow, or I could be healed a year from now. I've learned to deal with the uncertainty by not looking into the future, at least as much as possible. My true tests of patience happen every day, every time I need to stand up, sit down, get dressed, get into bed, walk, or sleep. There's not much I can do anymore that doesn't require severe concentration and strength of my arms and just pure will. I have had to learn to do everything differently and slowly so as not to fall or cause pain. Sometimes I still catch myself saying

"I'm going to run to the restroom real quick," and inside I crack myself up. I don't do anything quickly anymore.

I find that getting dressed is where I get the most impatient. Especially putting on socks or shoes. I need to use one hand to hold my leg up and use the other hand to slip on my sock and shoe. When was the last time you put a sock on with one hand. The sock keeps wanting to slide in between my toes and I have to keep starting over. Sometimes in exasperation I think, *Why?! Why God?! Why do we have toes?!* I've gotten better with practice, but it still takes me a few attempts.

When I think of how easily I used to do it, I begin feeling angry. That's my cue that I need to pause, take a deep breath, and give thanks to God for that moment. Because when I am grateful, I am reminded of my trust, and with trust, comes peace, and with peace, my patience will return. I can be patient because I know this suffering will not last forever. It will come to an end eventually. Each day I pray with conviction that God can save me, and hope that He will.

I may not be able to control my current situation, but I can control how I am choosing to live through it. Because that is exactly what it is, it is a choice. When you intentionally surrender to God's will, truly trust Him with your future, that's where you can find gratitude. And once you have gratitude, you have peace. And peace is what allows you to experience suffering with grace and patience. From my experience, patience is a necessity when you're going through any kind of suffering, whether it's financial, physical, or emotional.

However, the last thing you feel when you've been told you have terminal cancer, or any devastating news, is gratitude. Jesus understands this. He's lived this. Before he was crucified, He reached out to his heavenly Father in desperation.

Mathew 26: 36-46 describes his anguish: Then Jesus went with his disciples to a place called Gethsemane, and he said to them, "Sit here while I go over there and pray." He took Peter and the two sons of Zebedee along with him, and he began to be sorrowful and troubled. Then he said to them, "My soul is overwhelmed with sorrow to the point of death. Stay here and keep watch with me." Going a little farther, he fell with his face to the ground and prayed, "My Father, if it is possible, may this cup be taken from me. Yet not as I will, but as you will."

Jesus is saying, please, God, save me from this. I fear what is to come. But I trust you.

It comforts me to know that Jesus understands that I don't want to be going through what I'm going through. It's uncomfortable. It's painful. It's terrifying. Yet, at the same time, even when I am at my lowest, I truly, in my heart, wish for God's will because that is what Jesus has taught us by his example. Just as Jesus trusted his Father completely, I endeavor to trust Him completely. When I step out of myself, when I think of all the other people's tragedies that have affected my life, I have no doubt that God will use my suffering for His good. Who knows how many lives could be changed for His glory because of my suffering. That in itself is comforting to me. That is inspiring to me. And that is when I am able to say prayers and feel deeply in my heart gratitude for my suffering and I can get on with the work of suffering.

When I consider all the different trials in my life, all the disappointments and tragedies, I can now discern glimpses of good emerging from each adversity. Though I didn't always offer thanks to God in the moment, I've come to appreciate the transformative power of gratitude, a practice I adopted in my 30s.

One story that profoundly influenced my perspective was that of Corrie Ten Boom, recounted in her autobiography "The Hiding Place." Amidst the horrors of surviving the holocaust and her time spent in the Ravensbruck concentration camp,

Corrie and her sister found solace in scripture. Corrie's sister snuck a tiny Bible into the camp and would quietly and secretly hold Bible studies in the barracks. In fact, during these sessions, many women developed a faith in God they had not had previously.

One of the scriptures they studied was 1 Thessalonians 5:16-18: "Rejoice always, pray continually, give thanks in all circumstances; for this is God's will for you in Christ Jesus."

Corrie and her sister were thrown into a barracks that was supposed to be for 40 people, and there were hundreds of women sharing it. They were stacked on top of each other. They had little to no food, no bathing capability, and they worked long grueling hours doing manual labor in the brutal cold of winter. And on top of that, there was a rampant case of lice spreading throughout the barracks. The women felt them crawling on their skin at night, biting them, leaving rashes and sores on their skin. And here was Corrie's sister teaching them all to give thanks for these circumstances, for the lice!

Later in the book Corrie describes an encounter with one of the guards after the war. She had spoken at a church service about the power and necessity of forgiveness, and afterwards, a guard from the camp approached her. She hadn't recognized him at first, but then she caught a look, something triggered a memory. All of the painful memories of the concentration camp resurfaced and filled her with hatred. As he stood before her, asking for her forgiveness, she prayed for God's divine intervention and He provided her the mercy she sought. Later, through conversation with him, she learned that the only reason the guards had not entered her barracks was because of the lice. Had they entered and become aware of the Bible studies, they surely would have been executed on the spot, and any of the other women who participated. The lice they detested yet expressed gratitude for saved their lives.

This narrative resonated with me deeply, prompting me to find gratitude amidst my own hardships. It wasn't hard to realize that if they could give thanks for lice, I could give thanks for our dire financial circumstances.

The Rise Before the Fall

Shortly after Erik and I married, we started acquiring properties. In 2000, we purchased our first home in Yucca Valley, which is in the high desert, roughly 30 minutes from Palm Springs. The benefit of moving to the outskirts of Palm Springs was house values were lower, therefore we were able to afford more square footage and more acreage for less money. It was very exciting for me because I had never made such a purchase before. In my mind, this would be our forever home. Just like I had spent my first 18 years in the house I grew up in, I longed for that sense of "home" again. Not just in the literal sense, but figuratively as well.

In 2002, it became apparent that if I wanted to raise my income, I needed to commute to Los Angeles for work. The desert litigation consisted mostly of personal injury and small contract disputes. The depositions were typically short and there weren't many of them. As an independent contractor, I wasn't paid a salary, I was paid by the page. More pages meant more money. I began contacting larger agencies in Los Angeles and found that I could work almost any day I wanted and there was no shortage of all-day jobs. The commute was a concern, but I reasoned that if I worked just three days a week, that would provide more than enough pages to produce a nice income.

By 2003, my career really started to take off. I was doing multi-day arbitrations, long and technical depositions, and my income was the reward. However, I hadn't been correct in my three-day theory, and the long commute was really wearing on me. I could easily spend five hours a day in traffic if I hit both morning and evening rush hours.

It sounds absurd to anyone who doesn't live in California. *Why on earth would anyone do that,* is what any sane person would ask. All I can say is that Erik and I were young and ambitious, prepared to work hard with a goal of retiring before we were 50. But it didn't take long to realize that I couldn't subject myself to the lunacy of that drive every week. Besides the hours I spent taking down the proceedings, I worked for hours every week editing transcripts, which ate up most of my weekends.

Thankfully I had family in Orange County, near Los Angeles, and they invited me to stay with them on the days I was working instead of driving back to the desert. Not only did it cut my drive time drastically, but it also provided an opportunity to get to know my Aunt Kay, cousin Arlana, cousin Greg and his wife, Denise. Before moving to California, I had only known of them from family pictures and stories handed down from my mother. Aunt Kay was my mom's sister, and being with Aunt Kay always filled the hole in my heart that my mother's death created.

Erik's business was also picking up speed. He specialized in kitchens and bathrooms but had also taken on a few total remodel jobs. The economy was booming, and with the rising housing prices, homeowners had almost instant equity in their houses, and they wanted to take advantage of that. Needless to say, more work meant he needed more workers. Anybody who has worked in the construction field will tell you that finding good, competent workers can be quite challenging, especially at this time.

One of the things I loved about Erik was he always wanted to hire the underdog, the guy that was struggling for some reason or another. I think perhaps he felt he was paying it forward. It had been his ex-wife's father that had given him a chance when he was just a kid and had been kicked out of his home. That was Erik's introduction to construction and the trades. Sadly, this practice didn't always work out and it often found him scrambling to find new people.

Where Erik excelled was in sales. But as much as he enjoyed his customers during the initial encounters, once the work would begin, people's quirks would come to light. We had customers who wanted to chat with our workers while they were working, delaying their progress; customers who couldn't make up their minds, delaying the progress. At the end of the day of dealing with quirky customers, incompetent workers, and delayed supplies, Erik often came home mentally exhausted, his patience level at empty.

On the weekends when I wasn't working on transcripts, to find some relaxation, we would take a drive up to Lake Arrowhead, a small lake community about 90 minutes from where we lived. The stark difference between Lake Arrowhead and Yucca Valley was like comparing Switzerland and Afghanistan.

Lake Arrowhead was like escaping to another world 3,500 feet in the air. It was hard to believe that in just a little over an hour's drive, you were surrounded by towering pine trees, beautiful blue sky not contaminated by smog, and chalet style houses. In the summertime it was easily 40 degrees cooler than the blazing desert, and in the wintertime it was fun to go see the snow. In other seasons we would take a leisurely drive up the windy scenic highway and go to The Village, an outlet shopping area located on the lake that included restaurants overlooking the deep blue water. All the shops were constructed as chalet style buildings. It became a place where we could lose ourselves in the beauty and serenity of nature. It was where we could breathe deeply and exhale.

In the spring of 2002, with both of our businesses booming, we explored the idea of purchasing a vacation home there. We originally thought of just a small cabin, perhaps an A-frame. When we met with a realtor, they introduced us to the idea of renting it out when we weren't going to be using it. We learned that the more sleeping capacity the house offered, the higher the rent would be. With that in mind, we found a nice house with three fireplaces, an amazing view from the back deck, and four bedrooms that could sleep 12 people if we furnished the family rooms with sofa sleepers.

As much as Erik and I liked the house, we agreed that it wasn't a house we would live in full time, but it was a great price and in really good shape. There wasn't any work that we would need to do it, which was a huge relief. And if we could rent it twice a month, it would almost pay for itself. It was an investment we told ourselves.

The plan to rent it was quickly tossed out after our first rental. Unbeknownst to us, our first renters were a group of teenagers who woke up our neighbors by screaming off the balcony in the middle of the night. Not only that, we were disappointed when we weren't able to use the house that weekend.

Since we were too busy to travel, this second house allowed us an escape to a different climate and different scenery. We actually enjoyed experiencing winter up on the mountain. The few times it snowed, we lit a fire in the fireplace, drank hot chocolate, and snuggled on the couch as we watched the large snowflakes fall outside our window. By the next day it melted and we were back to work.

In 2004, Erik and I were casually driving around the lake area one weekend, and we stumbled upon an open house. We had a fondness for open houses and exploring new layouts and amenities, even though we weren't actively looking to buy. Initially, the house didn't impress us from the front view -- a 3-car garage and a short wooden walkway leading to an unremarkable front door. However, the true spectacle awaited inside.

Upon entering, our gaze was immediately drawn to the back wall adorned with floor-to-ceiling windows, offering a breathtaking view of an expansive deck nestled amidst pine trees. The spacious kitchen boasted a slate floor, complemented by beautiful wood flooring throughout the first level. A custom brick fireplace adorned one wall, enhancing the open layout that allowed for a panoramic view of the entire first floor—a truly stunning sight.

The rest of the house continued to exceed our expectations. Spread across five levels, each one left us in awe. Within the 4,500 square-foot space, we found three bedrooms, three and a half bathrooms, a lavish master bathroom featuring a two-sided fireplace, two offices, and a meticulously maintained wine room with humidity control.

Erik and I were astounded by the sheer magnitude of the house—it seemed to unfold endlessly before us. Every level, every room evoked a sense of wonder and amazement. While I found myself enchanted by the floor-to-ceiling windows on the top floor and the allure of the wine room, Erik was particularly drawn to the final level. Descending the last set of stairs led us to a fully-equipped movie theatre, complete with a projector-ready ceiling and a wall primed for a giant screen.

We walked out of that house in shock. The sellers were eager to sell and so the price was way below what they should have been asking for it. We had to buy this house! But now we had a dilemma. It was double the price of the house we just bought. Moreover, this wasn't just a vacation home; it would become our primary residence if we chose to move. Did we want to move to the mountains full time? Complicating matters further, we had recently purchased a court reporting agency, adding another layer of responsibility to our plate. Additionally, we still owned the Yucca Valley house. And, most importantly, Tyler, who was 11 years old, was living with us full time now and so he would need to switch schools. It would also increase our drive every other weekend for transporting him to his mother's.

Erik and I decided to go to the Lake Arrowhead Village, to our favorite Mexican restaurant so we could discuss all of this over some margaritas. We knew we were going to have to be creative if we decided to buy this house, and nothing makes you more creative than a pitcher of margaritas.

By the time our glasses were empty, we had devised a plan. We would sell our current Lake Arrowhead residence, utilizing the equity we had accrued in just two years—equivalent to a third of the new house's cost—to pay off the loan for the court reporting agency. That would clear two loans from our credit report. I urged Erik to sell our Yucca Valley house but he just wouldn't budge. His emotional attachment stemming from the amount of work he put into it clouded his judgement, but he did promise to make more of an effort to get it rented.

That same afternoon Erik contacted the realtor and told them we wanted to make an offer. Because of the new banking rules and the current housing market, we felt confident that we could get a loan for what we were now calling our "dream home." Thanks to the owners' eagerness, they accepted our offer and we put the wheels in motion to get our other house sold.

After we signed the papers for our "dream home," our realtor congratulated us but then threw us a bit of a curve ball.

"Okay, now that we're officially closed, I have something to tell you," she said. Both Erik and I looked at her inquisitively.

We had some practice now on signing closing documents and no one had ever said anything like that to us before.

"There was another family that wanted to put an offer on the house but yours had been presented first and accepted and so I was legally forbidden to tell the sellers about the second offer. Now that it has closed, the family wanted me to convey the offer to you. They are willing to pay $100,000 over what you just paid for the house."

Erik and I sat there dumbfounded. Erik wanted to make sure he was hearing it right. "You mean we could sell this house to them right now and they will give us $100,000 more than what we bought it for."

"Yes."

Again we sat there, stunned. We looked at each other, trying to read each other's thoughts. I thought of those windows and the views. I'm sure Erik was thinking of the movie theatre. "It's our dream home," I said.

"Tell them we're sorry, we're going to keep the house." Erik told the realtor. I smiled a huge smile. I was so proud of Erik for not just going for the money grab. Looking back now, I pound my forehead with my fist and say, "Stupid. Stupid. Stupid." It was a great house but it was just a house. Today, if you asked me what my "dream home" is, I would tell you it's the one that's paid off.

I can't say that I didn't enjoy the house. The summer days when I wasn't working and I was able to lay on a chaise on the upper deck, basking in the warm sun and soaking up the serenity of the forest, were heavenly. The winter days that it snowed and we had a fire blazing in the fireplace as we watched our local squirrel jump from tree to tree collecting branches for its nest were tranquil. I just wish there had been more of those days.

The following two years, as the housing bubble steadily inflated, Erik's business was busier than ever before. His days were filled with visiting ongoing remodels to check the progress and quality of the work, picking up supplies, and meeting with new customers at different stores to pick out tile or appliances. Evenings and weekends were often spent at potential customers' homes going over bids and selling. This left little time for relaxing and decompression, but Erik realized that this bubble wouldn't last forever and he wanted to capitalize on it.

One of the things that attracted me to Erik was his ambition and work ethic. That first summer we were together in Minnesota, he began mapping out our future and explaining how we could retire early if we worked hard and were smart with our money. As someone who knew nothing about investing or money management, this was incredibly appealing to me. Through the years, he read book after book on being successful and building wealth. I soon felt comfortable and a bit relieved that I could leave our financial future in his hands. I trusted him completely.

However, after we moved into our "dream home," I began to notice that as fast as money was coming in, it was going out. First, it was items for the new house: a brand-new pool table, movie screen and projector, exercise equipment for a home gym. Then it was a restored 1956 Chevy and ultimately a weeklong timeshare of a houseboat on Lake Powell. Perhaps he was trying to purchase relaxation, but that wasn't the result it produced. Other than watching movies and our yearly houseboat trip, the other items collected dust and Erik was constantly on edge. I noticed that the more successful Erik became, the more he wanted to show it off to others. And no matter how much we had, it was never enough.

In the spring of 2006, Erik was introduced to the book "Rich Dad Poor Dad" by Robert Kiyosaki. It proposes money secrets that rich parents tell their kids that the poor and middle class don't know about. There is even a board game that we became infatuated with called Cashflow. It's like Monopoly but on steroids. It boasts that it simulates real life scenarios allowing players to learn strategies and skills necessary to achieve financial independence. We played it often and tried to absorb all that we thought it could teach us.

That summer, while visiting a local salon in Lake Arrowhead, my stylist, Lisa, mentioned that the owner of the salon was looking to sell. My ears perked up. This was what the Cashflow game was all about, recognizing financial opportunities. I inquired how many stylists rented space from him, how much they were paying him, what she thought the monthly lease was, and how much he was asking. From just the preliminary questions, it was intriguing. It appeared to have a good ROI (return on investment), and with each stylist in charge of their own clients, they were independent contractors. Since my court reporters were all independent contractors, I was familiar and comfortable with the arrangement. When I told Erik about the salon, he was instantly intrigued. Within a week he met with the salon owner and they hammered out a deal for us to purchase the salon.

Initially, our vision for the salon acquisition was modest – maintaining the existing space, possibly enhancing marketing efforts, without foreseeing it becoming a full-time commitment. However, Erik's perspective diverged. Even before finalizing the salon purchase, he envisioned relocating to a larger property, potentially integrating it with his remodeling company, expanding our assets. Though apprehensive about adding another venture to our already bustling lives, Erik's confidence and track record persuaded me to trust his instincts. After all, our previous successes were largely attributed to his foresight and acumen. He was so much smarter than I was when it came to all of this. As I used to tell people who tried to congratulate me on any of our success, "It's all Erik. I'm just along for the ride."

By the fall of 2006, Erik found what he thought was the perfect space for the salon even though we hadn't officially closed on the salon yet. That concerned me because it felt like we were putting the cart before the horse. Suddenly, the owner of the salon was pulling back, starting to ask for more. After several more rounds of negotiations, Erik had had it and called the whole thing off. I was actually feeling relieved but Erik still wanted to purchase the building and put our own salon in there along with his remodel business. In fact, Erik concluded there was enough room in this building to open a spa and salon. This bothered me on so many levels:

1. What did we know about running a salon or a spa?

2. What about all this talk about the housing bubble bursting?

3. This building was the most expensive building we had ever purchased and would require all the equity we had in our dream home, which would raise our mortgage payment.

4. How would we finance the complete remodel that was going to be required?

For every concern, Erik had a plausible answer.

1. Since the stylists would be independent contractors, once we got it up and running, it wouldn't require much of our time.

2. We would be fine if the bubble burst. One kitchen sale from each location would cover the mortgages.

3. The equity in the house was doing us no good just sitting there. Financial success was all about leverage.

4. Erik would do most of the work himself on the remodel and so it would just be the cost of materials, of which he could get discounts because of his contacts.

Despite the pit in my stomach, I agreed. My intuition was working overtime trying to warn me and I ignored it. I told myself it was just fear, that I needed to trust Erik. But I was the one paying the bills and this would bring our monthly mortgage nut to $20,000.

After we closed on the new salon building, we got into our car.

"Are you hungry? Let's just grab some burgers and fries on the way home."

I wouldn't usually partake in his fast-food indulgences, but I was stressed beyond the max and nothing sounded better than a greasy burger and french fries. As we pulled up to the menu, Erik asked me, "Do you have any cash?"

"I'll check but I don't think so."

Nope, no cash.

"Either do I," Erik said. "How about a credit card?"

"They're all maxed out."

"You don't have any change at all?"

I dug down to the bottom of my purse and found some quarters. Erik dove into this center console and found a few more coins. We could afford one hamburger.

Erik joked, "How did we just get a loan for a million dollars when we can't afford two hamburgers."

And that pretty much explains the housing bubble. In a nutshell, banks were lending money to people who should not have been given loans. Ourselves included.

The salon project still makes me shake my head and laugh when I look back on it. What the heck were we thinking? The amount of work needed to open a functioning spa/salon was staggering: The whole building would have to be gutted, plumbing added for the sinks, furniture and equipment purchased, and then the task of finding stylists and massage therapists.

Had we opened a spa in the valley, meaning not on the mountain, the pool of applicants would have been plentiful. The population in Lake Arrowhead in 2006 was probably less than 10,000 people. It was very slim pickings for these positions. Our plan was to put in six hair stations and charge $1,000 per station. That alone would pay the mortgage. Any income from the massage therapists and nail tech, plus any products we sold, would be profit.

The first problem we encountered was we couldn't find any hairdressers that wanted to rent a chair. They all wanted to be employees and get paid hourly. I saw that as a huge problem, but Erik got out his calculator, his favorite toy, and started running the numbers on what each stylist could bring in. If we could get the people in the door and sell more than one service, it could potentially be more lucrative for us. He wasn't deterred at all.

The following months as Erik continued with the remodel, I allocated any free time to searching for stylists, acquiring all the necessary furniture, and learning our new salon software. Weekends were spent assembling Ikea furniture and shelving and shopping for products to fill the shelves. Opening our American Express bill was the most dreaded and terrifying experience that month. The $40,000 balance somehow managed to punch me right in the gut.

Then Erik decided we needed a water feature.

"What?" I thought I either heard wrong or he was joking.

"The backyard would be perfect. I've got the perfect spot. It already has a slope so we could put a waterfall and little stream, with a bench or a small table and chairs, and people could hang out there in between services. It would be so calming and relaxing."

I finally had to speak up. "I won't argue that it would be nice, but how much is that going to cost us? I don't think it's wise to do it at this time. Let's get the spa up and running and make sure it's going to be successful."

The following week we had a team of men digging the outline for our new waterfall. It was frustrating to me that Erik wouldn't listen to me sometimes, but he could be like a dog with a bone, and when he was fixated on something, he made it happen. I just kept telling myself that it would all work out, that Erik knew what he was doing.

Thank you, God, for making Erik so fearless. Thank you for this new opportunity and for all that we can learn from it.

The salon/spa was set to open July 4th weekend of 2007. It had been a long and arduous project but Erik did a beautiful job. He had worked closely with his cousin Kris, who was an interior decorator. What used to be a dark and dingy building became bright and inviting. It was full of mountain charm and comfort. Everybody that came in raved about it. We were all excited about the opening, and I was really looking forward to seeing money come in the door instead of going out.

Red Rock Retreat

That summer of 2007 I was looking forward to the houseboat week like it was a life preserver. I willed myself to just keep going, rising from bed at 4 a.m. to work on transcripts before commuting to LA, staying up late to finish transcripts, spending my off days either at the salon or my agency. Weekends were split between the salon and catching up on laundry. A day off? What was that?

By the time August arrived, the salon was operating but not making nearly the money we were hoping. Additionally, we were dealing with employees now and so we had the typical employee problems; people not showing up for their shift, stealing product from us, etc. As we packed up for the long drive to our houseboat vacation, however, I felt reasonably confident that it could run for a week with no issues. Well, I was somewhat confident. I was slightly confident. Okay, I had no friggin clue if it could or not but I just really didn't care.

As I buckled my seatbelt in Erik's red F250, with Tyler in the backseat and all of our luggage secured tightly in the bed of the truck, I exhaled. We had done it. I had never been more grateful for his persistence in getting this houseboat share. Truth be told, we would not be taking this vacation had it not already been paid for. It was good that it forced us to take this week off.

Thank you, God, for giving Erik the insight to make this purchase. Please be with us the whole trip, keep us safe, and please help Erik to relax and let go of his frustrations.

Our first stop was in Las Vegas. We would stay the night there and then finish the drive in the morning. It wasn't exactly halfway but we enjoyed Vegas every now and then. We liked to stay at different hotels for the different experiences, and that summer we were staying at the Bellagio. It's a beautiful hotel with a magnificent pool area. As I started digging into my suitcase to find my bathing suit, my phone rang. It was Lori, the one stylist that we employed that I trusted. *Crap. Why is she calling me?* For a second I contemplated not answering but my conscience wouldn't allow it.

"Hi Lori, what's up?" I said, trying not to let the annoyance and dread I was feeling be reflected in my voice.

"Um, do you have a few minutes?"

I looked at Erik and told him to take Tyler to the pool.

"Yep, sure. What's going on?" *We haven't even been gone 24 hours. What could possibly have happened?*

"So, um, Jackie (our nail tech) had a mani/pedi client this morning. I guess she offered the client some wine and they -- well, um, they pretty much got drunk. Jackie forgot to turn off the water to the pedi tub and it overflowed into the room. But that's okay. We got it all cleaned up. But now it's not working. Which is fine. We can wait until you get back to fix it."

I started to rub my forehead in defeat and exhaustion.

"But, um, just now we had a visit from a man who was really upset. Apparently, he's the husband of Jackie's client, and unbeknownst to Jackie, she is an alcoholic. He's furious that we gave her wine. We told him we didn't know, that it wasn't our fault. He wanted to talk to the owners but we told him that you were out of town, so, um, you might hear from him when you get back."

This is just perfect.

"Tell Jackie to cancel any clients she has scheduled while we're gone." I said. I couldn't trust what else she might do.

"I already did. I hope you don't mind."

Thank you, God, for Lori.

"Not at all. I'm glad someone there has their head on straight. Thanks for the call and the heads-up. Nothing I can do about it now, but it was good you called."

"I'm so sorry, Kathy, that I had to call you. Go and enjoy your week and don't worry about us at all. I'll keep everyone in line."

"Lori, thank you. I don't know what I'd do without you." I hung up the phone and said a prayer of gratitude that I would have no cell service once we got on the lake. I was looking forward to a week of blissful ignorance.

The houseboat, christened the Red Rock Retreat, stretched out to a length of 75 feet with three bedrooms and two bathrooms. Complete with air conditioning, a dishwasher, and even a waterslide, it provided a comfortable oasis amidst the rugged terrain. Its upper deck offered lounge chairs and a wet bar, creating an ideal spot for basking in the sun, while a convenient console allowed for steering on high. It wasn't luxurious but it was nice, clean, and kept up well.

Lake Powell is an artificial reservoir on the Colorado River in Arizona and Utah. It's the second largest in the United States. It is vastly different than the lakes I grew up around. Lake Powell is in the middle of a desert and it is surrounded by towering red rock formations. As you travel down the lake, you can observe where previous water levels have left their mark on the steep walls. The one thing this lake has in common with Minnesota lakes is the feeling of tranquility that they inspire. The houseboat was truly one of the best adventures of my life.

After we were all loaded and unpacked and safely out of the marina, Erik at the helm on the top deck, me sitting on the cushioned bench next to him, the warm gentle breeze kissed our faces as we made our way through the first canyon, away from civilization. Just the thought of the week ahead without any work, without any itinerary, without any deadlines, made me feel giddy. I could feel the stress dissipate like a heavy fog lifting. I allowed my mind to settle, and I gently pushed away thoughts of concern for the salon, for our businesses, for the future. I had to reset my mindset.

God, I thank you so much for this time and for our ability to do this trip and for Dawn being able to join us. Thank you for being so present and so loving. Please surround us this whole week with your Holy Spirit and peace.

One might think we would run out of things to do, that we would become bored. Actually, that was precisely the allure.

Oh, how I longed for the luxury of idleness, freedom from obligations. The beauty of a houseboat was there was as much or as little boredom as you chose to embrace. There were no dinner reservations we had to rush to. Want to sleep in? Great. Want to rise early and view a spectacular sunrise from the top deck with a hot cup of coffee? Wonderful! I'll see you there! We existed in the moment and we absorbed all of the carefree feelings we could, as if we could hold them inside and bring them home with us.

The casual days passed slowly and quickly at the same time. Each evening, we congregated on the top deck with our glasses of wine, ready to stargaze. As an extra perk, there was a meteor shower forecasted and we had front row seats to nature's grand fireworks display. As soon as the sun settled behind the tall rocks, we were all on our chaise lounge chairs with our faces fixed on the clear sky. With no city lights to contend with, the sky was deep black but peppered generously with bright stars. We marveled at the brightness and the volume of stars that filled the sky and we easily pointed out the Milky Way. Suddenly a stream of light would shoot across the sky, impossible to overlook, and we would all erupt with excitement. If shooting stars were drawn with a fine tip, these were drawn in bold. And they were everywhere. All night long was a cacophony of oohs and ahs, wows, and did-you-see-that-ones.

When we weren't wakeboarding and skiing, we loved to take our speedboat and explore the labyrinthine channels and hidden coves that the enormous lake offered. We were in awe of the towering cliffs that enclosed both sides of the boat as we meandered through the clear, still water. Often we found secluded beaches that demanded we pull our boat up to so that we could put our feet in the soft red sand and swim in the fresh water.

Erik, Tyler, Dawn, and I swam and laughed and yelled up echoes to the surrounding walls of steep rock.

"Hello!!" Hello, hello, hello.

"Luke!" Luke, Luke, Luke. "I am your father!" Father, father, father.

We all laughed like children. Because for that brief moment and many other brief moments throughout the week, we got to be kids again. There is no greater relief from the struggles and stresses of adulthood than being able to recapture a small part of your youth.

The best part about a houseboat vacation is reconnecting with the people we came with. It's unfortunate how you can live with someone and see them every day and yet still feel apart from them. Busy schedules can be a silent killer of relationships. The time spent on the top deck in the early mornings, exploring the quiet channels in the afternoons, preparing meals together, and our evening stargazes offered us opportunities to have real conversations. For Dawn and I, we didn't just catch up on our lives, we enjoyed meaningful conversations leisurely, allowing us time to reflect on the topic before contributing. Erik and I were able to talk about things other than work and financial strategies. Tyler had our full attention without any interruptions.

For the ride back to the marina, I attempted to soak in every last bit of sunshine and peacefulness that I could. If it were possible, I would have filled every pocket with it so that I could bring it home.

The Beginning of the End

Not long after we returned from Lake Powell, we started what we call fire season in California. The drought that had been ravaging California left a lot of good tinder for fires. It was frustrating when fires were caused by careless people throwing cigarettes out their window, but it was infuriating to learn that people were setting them on purpose.

Erik and I were back to work. I was back to juggling my agency, my own depo work, and the salon, although the salon was at the bottom of my list. After taking a week off, I needed some fast income. Being a freelance court reporter affords you the ability to take off whenever you like but it doesn't pay for the time off. I knew the salon needed my attention but I needed a quick fix. We had $20,000 in mortgages to pay. The salon was going to have to wait.

At the end of October, while I was at a deposition, Erik called me. I was glad we were on a break and I could pick up. I had been hearing reports that there were possibly fires in the area of our dream home.

"Hey," I said.

"Hey. I just wanted you to know we're being evacuated. I had one of the guys bring the box van up here, and we're loading it up with stuff that we don't want to lose. We've grabbed all the photos, your jewelry box, I packed some of your clothes, and we've taken framed photos and some of the art off the walls. Is there anything else you can think of that we should take?"

"Oh, my gosh. Do you really think it could reach our house?"

"Right now there are embers bigger than playing cards landing on our house. It's not good."

"Go into the office and grab all the files that say insurance or that look important."

"Got it. Okay, we gotta go. Call me when you're done."

I felt sick to my stomach as I hung up the phone. We resumed the deposition and I wrote word for word what everybody was saying but I wasn't paying attention to any of it. It's amazing how our brains work. If somebody had asked me to read their last question or answer back, I could have easily done so without any memory of writing it. In fact, it wasn't uncommon for my mind to wander, thinking what I should make for dinner or my grocery list.

That day, however, I was not thinking about dinner or grocery shopping, I was hoping and praying that our house would still be standing at the end of the day. By the time we finished, I was completely nauseous. Fires were not a new occurrence in the mountains, but it had never been this close to home, literally. When I called Erik back, he and his best buddy JR were at Harley's, the pub down the street from our office. He said that there were confirmed houses that had been burned to the ground. They didn't know the addresses yet.

In California, wildfires are as common as hurricanes in Florida and so they too are given names just as hurricanes are. This fire is what would be known as the Grass Valley fire. This name was chosen for the location of where the fire was thought to have originated from. In this case, a tree had fallen on a power line, throwing sparks into a forest dried from drought and a bark beetle infestation. The Santa Ana winds then ignited the sparks into flames and spread the fire quickly and forcefully throughout the mountain. Some houses were in the path of the fire, some fell victim to falling embers, and some were next door to burning structures. Just in our small area, nearly 200 homes were burned to the ground. Of course, I wouldn't find that out until later. All I knew was practically the whole mountain was evacuated with no idea for how long, and we may or may not have our dream home or the salon when the day is over.

By the time my deposition was over, practically the whole mountain had been evacuated and without any idea as to duration. Since schools were closed, Tyler went to stay with his mom. Thankfully, Erik and I and Taffy were invited to stay in the guest room above a garage of a client of Erik's.

Erik had just completed a full remodel on their beautiful house in Yucaipa and we happily accepted when they offered it to us. They were very hospitable, and we were very grateful for a place to stay. It just so happened that the couple we were staying with was a retired police chief and so he had the proper connections to allow Erik up the mountain after the fire had been tamed. The mountain had remained closed to traffic because of the potential of looters. Looting had been a problem in the past, degenerates who take advantage of empty homes, and so the police were doing everything they could to thwart those attempts.

Erik called me when they got up to our house. I was mentally preparing myself for the worst news. *It's going to be fine. It's just a house. God will guide us through it.*

"The house is fine! I can't believe it!" Erik exclaimed.

I gave a huge sigh of relief. Thank you, God!

"And the salon?" I asked.

"That's okay too! But you wouldn't believe the devastation that we've seen. So many homes just gone, smoldering. It's so sad." Erik said.

Oh, God, please be with those families that lost their homes.

"We got so lucky; I can't believe it." I said.

Even though the fires were out, it was a few weeks before we could return to the mountain. The fire destroyed mostly homes, but it also affected businesses in the mountain communities. They didn't burn down, but being forced to close for several weeks, and then the lack of business afterwards made it difficult for many to remain open. Because of the fire, the tourists weren't visiting as they had before. It was also starting to get cold and peak season for tourists had come to an end. We continued to struggle through the rest of 2007. We were able to collect some insurance for the days the business was forced to close, but it was nowhere near enough to keep the business going.

Erik's work began to show signs of decline, as was my agency. When we purchased the agency, I voiced my concerns to Erik about being an owner versus a reporter. Owning a court reporting agency requires an ability to effectively sell and schmooze. It is a fiercely competitive field and very dependent on building relationships. Erik promised that he could fill that role for me and so I reluctantly agreed.

However, after the sale went through, neither of us had the time necessary to attract new clients or foster goodwill to keep the ones we had. My agency then became the Titanic, slowly sinking, barely noticeable at first. I knew we were losing clients and revenue but I felt powerless to do anything about it. By 2008, the boat was vertical in the water and beginning its final descent into the abyss.

By March of 2008 it was clear that we were going to have to make some choices. The money just wasn't there to pay all our debts. Stress was at an all-time high. I kept thinking of Corrie Ten Boom and the lice.

Thank you, God, for all of this. I don't know why this is happening to us, but I know you will use it for our good. I trust you, God.

These prayers brought me peace and patience. They reminded me that nothing was more important than our families and friends. Houses and possessions could all be replaced.

Erik, on the other hand, was not so peaceful. I knew he was making great efforts to keep himself in check, but there were times that he just couldn't contain it and he would erupt. During one such rant in rage he proclaimed, "I want a divorce!"

What? What do you mean you want a divorce? The statement was preposterous to me.

"Too bad," I spat back. I knew it was the anger and not how he truly felt. It was preposterous to me because I knew we had a good marriage. I knew we loved each other.

"Why aren't you upset about all this? Why doesn't it bother you?" He screamed at me, referring to our current financial situation.

"You know why," I said calmly. And he did. I tried telling him that God had a plan, we just needed to trust Him, but he wanted nothing to do with that conversation and so I stopped trying to get him to understand. Instead, I prayed, *God, I know you love Erik so much. Help him to feel your presence in all of this. Please use this to bring Erik closer to you. Bring him peace, Lord. I know your promise to us*:

> Jeremiah 29:11: "For I know the plans I have for you," declares the Lord, "plans to prosper you and not to harm you, plans to give you hope and a future."

One Saturday in March of 2008 Erik told me that he wanted to go to church the next day. I was shocked and ecstatic! We were still living on the mountain at that time, but we hadn't attended any of the churches. We chose a Presbyterian church since that had been the denomination I attended as a child. It was a beautiful log cabin style church with lots of wooden detail and stained glass. That Sunday when we entered the church, I had such a good feeling, like God was walking in alongside us, with a hand on each of our backs, guiding us. I let the organ music of old and favorite hymns envelope me. I was blanketed with a warm and familiar feeling.

At some point during the service they read a scripture that resonated loudly with me and became etched in my mind:

Romans 5:1-5: "Therefore, since we have been justified through faith, we have peace with God through our Lord Jesus Christ, through whom we have gained access by faith into this grace in which we now stand. And we boast in the hope of the glory of God. Not only so, but we also glory in our sufferings, because we know that suffering produces perseverance; perseverance, character; and character, hope. And hope does not put us to shame, because God's love has been poured out into our hearts through the Holy Spirit, who has been given to us."

When I heard this, I had no doubt that God had directed us to that church, on that day, that morning, through Erik, to hear those words. Memorizing scripture has never been a practice of mine, and yet this one has been permanently pressed into my heart. The idea of not only thanking God for our suffering but finding glory in it. Yes, suffering ultimately leads to hope, but it seems to me that in order to glory in anything, you have to first appreciate it, be grateful for it. Once you can honestly, humbly, sincerely thank God for whatever it is that you are suffering from or because of, glory can now be available to you.

I also believe that finding glory in suffering is not so much because of circumstances causing the suffering, it is our complete and utter dependence on God for our life. It is the closeness we feel to Jesus. It is more than a prayer, it is falling at His feet in total surrender. That is the glory.

The following months were difficult, and it was just the beginning. By April 2008, the salon was closed and the bank foreclosed. Work was almost nonexistent for Erik. People were in full-blown panic mode and holding tight to their purses. Even the people who had money were deciding that their new kitchen remodel could wait a bit longer because they were watching their stock investments and retirement accounts shrink smaller and smaller by the day. Erik tried everything he could to stir up business. He cut his prices so much he would have barely made anything, but it would have been SOMETHING. Still no sales. Erik had clients that were in the middle of their remodel and using HELOC funds to pay for it and the bank shut off the money spigot. They simply said, no more. It left the families scrambling to figure out a way to pay their balances and finish the jobs.

Lucky for us we live in a very litigious country and there is no shortage of lawsuits and depositions and so I had as much work as I could take. While I was working more than ever, Erik found himself with lots of time on his hands. And so even though Erik was not much of a drinker, it was not uncommon for me to call him on my way home from Los Angeles and he would be with JR at Harley's. I would stop there to pick him up on my way home and join them at the run-down pub for a glass of mediocre red wine. The conversation was almost the same every day.

"Did you hear about [insert contractor name]?" JR would say. "He's the [insert building trade] guy that was on my last job. He's getting divorced. His wife left him after he lost the business and their house. Had to file bankruptcy."

JR and his wife were the only other couple we knew who made it through this nightmare with their relationship intact, if not stronger. All the other contractors we knew lost their businesses, their homes, and their spouses. It was heartbreaking.

By the summer of 2008, Erik was filled with defeat. He would park himself in front of Fox News and stare at it for hours. He stopped going into the office. I was still going to the office daily on my way to or from Los Angeles. I was always juggling bills and running payroll for the agency. It broke my heart that I didn't know how to help him, and, frankly, I didn't have time to figure it out.

One of the perks about our companies sharing office space was we were able to employ one receptionist/office manager. It had been an arduous process to find the right person, but I knew within a very short time of meeting Robin that she was going to be a good fit. Throughout the next couple of years, she became a valuable member of both our businesses, as well as a cherished friend. When we went to Lake Powell, we left her in charge of my business, Erik's business, and our dog.

Erik had a few remaining remodels going, but by this point he had checked out emotionally and mentally. It was all just too much, to see all his hard work the past 10 years going down the drain. His workers started calling me when Erik wouldn't answer his phone. They had questions and decisions that needed to be made and didn't know who else to call. I was tempted to get angry at Erik but how could I? I understood why he was feeling and behaving this way. He had been the one spearheading all our financial endeavors. How often had he heard from me, "I'm just along for the ride." I'm sure he felt responsible for our present financial downward spiral. My intent had been to give Erik all the credit, but instead I saddled him with all the blame.

I began getting to the office earlier in the morning so that I could meet with Erik's foreman. We would sit down together and go over the status of the remaining jobs that we had going and the best way to go about getting them finished. I valued his input and his knowledge, and we couldn't have finished those jobs without him. We eventually finished up all the jobs and the warehouse was empty for the first time since we had purchased it.

Thank you, God, so much for Ray and his loyalty and help. Please bless him and his family during this difficult time.

One afternoon as I was finishing up a deposition and packing up my equipment, I received a call from Erik. "I'm done, Kathy! I'm done! I'm driving down the mountain and I'm going to drive my truck off the mountain!"

My stomach did a summersault and I felt bile up in my throat. "Erik! No! You can't do that!"

"I can't fucking take it, Kathy. I can't take it anymore."

Tears were making it hard for me to see. I was trying to finish packing up as fast as I could but my hands were shaking so much, I was having difficulty. "Honey, stop, it's going to be okay. Just go to the office. I'll meet you there. It's going to be okay. I promise!"

Silence.

"Erik?"

"I'll see you later."

I looked at my phone. He had hung up. *Please, God, no, no, no. Be with Erik right now. Please God help him. Don't let him do this.*

My trembling hands called Robin. As soon as she answered, I managed to squeak out, "Robin, can you get me the number for a suicide hot line?"

"Kathy, what's wrong? What's going on?"

"I think Erik is going to kill himself."

"Oh, my God."

Robin gave me the number and I called and they walked me through some things I could say. I sped to the office, hoping that he would meet me there. The whole way to the office I kept trying to call him. Finally he answered. He was okay. He was with JR, and they were commiserating at Harley's. *Thank you, God.* I knew JR would talk him off the ledge.

Shortly after that I made an appointment with a counselor. Money was tight so we saw a woman who was in training for a reduced price. I didn't give Erik a choice, he was going. He knew I was serious when I informed him, and he didn't put up a fight. I didn't have any experience with therapists other than Jerry, the father that I nannied for, and so I wasn't sure what to expect. In my mind I was hoping for a Jerry, somebody who had a way of making you feel like a friend immediately, easy to talk to.

The woman was younger than I anticipated, perhaps in her mid-20s. Both Erik and I felt a little uncomfortable with the fact she was practically his daughter's age, and she didn't do much to put us at ease. She started with some basic questions, easy answers. Erik and were sitting next to each other, holding hands, and she noted that, and that it was indicative of a healthy marriage.

One helpful observation I made was that it was easier to tell her something that was bothering me than it was to tell Erik. It felt safe. We talked about how his declaration of divorce made me feel. Even though we both knew he didn't mean it, it was hurtful and not acceptable. We touched on the threat he made on the mountain, and Erik explained it was a moment of rage but that he would never take his own life. Having experienced enough of his angry eruptions, I agreed with him, I didn't believe that he would ever hurt anyone else or himself.

Erik was not a quitter. He began to explore other options for work. Since his whole adult life had revolved around construction, he decided that he needed to think outside of the box.

Epoxy and Puppies

2008 was the summer of epoxy countertops and flooring. Erik had a contractor friend named Sherri. She was a lovely older woman with a very caring nature and Erik was very drawn to her motherly demeanor. Through Sherri, he was introduced to epoxy countertops. The benefits to epoxy were it was cheaper than stone and they were custom-made. Sherri touted it as a great time to get into this business because people were looking for less expensive ways to redo their kitchen. She demonstrated the process to Erik and his creative nature was sparked. This particular endeavor I didn't know about until he informed me of his upcoming classes to learn the process. The workshop was $350. *Okay, that's reasonable.* I was happy that he found something to occupy his time and he clearly enjoyed the innovative aspect of the work.

Upon completing the workshop and before he had sold a single countertop, unbeknownst to me, Erik decided to become a distributor. Somehow he mentioned it casually in conversation and I had to take a pause. "Wait," I said, "how much was it to become a distributor?"

"It was only $5,000, but also included a bunch of supplies." My ears were ringing. *Only $5,000.*

I deflated like a balloon. What could I do? It was already done. Over the next few months he sold one countertop and one deck floor. Then that toy was put aside and forgotten about.

God, thank you for giving Erik the courage to try something new. Please guide him and show him what to do next.

This was the same time I began the process of prioritizing our debts. Since we were basically down to just my income, I was bringing in more than any other time in my life but it wasn't nearly enough to keep all the balls in the air that we were juggling.

Priority No. 1 was a roof over our head. Where was the cheapest place to live? Yucca Valley. Even though we had robbed every cent of equity from it, it had the lowest mortgage payment. Our dream home would have to go.

And people have always asked me, "Why didn't you sell it?"

The answer is easy. Nobody was buying houses. Nobody. We knew we could never sell it for what we owed on it.

As soon as that decision was made, I stopped making the mortgage payments on it. In all honesty, the banks were so flooded with foreclosures, and without the proper resources to enforce them, we probably could have stayed in the dream home for a year before we would officially be kicked out. I knew many people who had quit paying their mortgage the year before and they were still occupying the home. They wouldn't say so, but it seemed to benefit the bank if they stayed. At least then the houses were being cared for, yards were staying maintained until the foreclosure could take place. I had heard multiple stories of houses sitting empty, squatters taking up residence, lawns becoming completely overgrown and an eyesore to the poor neighbors who had been able to keep their homes. We decided to move back down to Yucca Valley in the fall, before the snowy weather started. Plus, living with the notion that we could be forced to leave at any moment sounded more like a nightmare than a dream.

After loading up the last box and backing out of the driveway for the last time, it was a melancholy drive down the mountain. It felt as though we weren't just leaving our dream home behind us, it was as if we had boxed up all our other dreams and we left them sitting in the empty garage. *God, I'm not feeling grateful at this moment, but I trust you and I thank you for this loss. I know you are going to use this somehow for your good.* At that time my gratitude was spoken through gritted teeth.

Priority No. 2 was transportation. We had to have our cars.

Priority No. 3 was food and incidentals.

Priority No. 4 was Erik's vendors. Most of those shops were small businesses that we had worked with for years. The owners and workers were our friends. I wouldn't let them down like so many other contractors had. Every bill and account were paid in full.

Thank you, God, for providing for our basic needs. Thank you for all that we are going through right now. I trust you, Lord.

After those priorities were accounted for, I had to decide which bills would go on the chopping block. I cancelled all our insurance except for auto. No more credit card payments, that was easy. I started calling the mortgage holders for our office space and our Yucca Valley home in the hopes of obtaining loan modifications. That itself was a major time commitment. I would wait an hour on hold just to have someone tell me to submit different documents and they would see what they could do. I would then spend evenings gathering all they requested, spend a half hour in front of a fax machine, and hear nothing back from them. That then required another call, another hour on hold, to then have someone tell us that that they didn't receive them, or that they now required other documents, or that there was nothing they could do. We spoke to an attorney about filing for bankruptcy but I was making too much money as a court reporter.

In the summer of 2009 Erik was online and looking at Akita puppies. Majesty, his first Akita, passed away the year prior, and he was saddened deeply from the loss. She had been a fiercely loyal dog, smart, and very loving. She had been with Erik for 10 years and he was missing the calmness that a canine companion provides. Of course I kept telling him, "No. I'm putting my foot down on this one."

"Why not?"

"Because we don't know where we're going to be living. Plus, we have Taffy. Isn't he enough? He's so easy. Do you remember what it's like to have a puppy?"

He knew I was making sense but there was that bone again and he wasn't about to give it up.

Knowing his mind was set on getting another dog, I tried to talk him into getting another breed. Perhaps a Golden Retriever. Majesty had been a great dog but he had forgotten about the responsibility of owning an Akita. They are very strong-willed and powerful dogs. They are also fiercely loyal, but usually just to their own family. Majesty would let Tosha and Tyler do whatever they wanted with her, even lay on her like a pillow. But when my 5-year-old niece tried to pet her back, she showed her teeth. Oftentimes we would put her in our bedroom if we were having anyone over she wasn't familiar with. When we introduced her to Taffy, at first she wouldn't even look at him. Then she attacked him. Erik had to pull her off him and dominate her. She eventually warmed up to Taffy when she realized he wasn't going anywhere, and they even began to play together. But I always worried that she would bite another dog, or worse, a person, and we would be sued. I was very reluctant to take on that burden again.

"I understand you miss Majesty, but if you must get another dog, let's get something that's more dog and person friendly."

It would fall on deaf ears. I mean that almost literally. It was like he didn't even hear me.

For months, he kept bringing it up and I would shoot it down. Absolutely not. Partly, I also felt that HIS puppy would become MY puppy and I didn't have time to take care of another one of his ideas.

"But it would be good for Taffy to have another dog around." He was ruthless in his sales pitch, knowing my weak spots. "And I could get another pure white one, just like Majesty."

"I'm not saying yes, but you can't get another pure white one. You'll expect her to be Majesty and you'll never have another Majesty. She'll be a different dog. She needs to have some color on her. But I'm not saying yes!"

Fall of 2009 rolled around and after dinner one night he brought me his computer. "I want to show you something." *Lord, please help me.*

On the screen he placed in front of me was a little white Akita fluff ball not more than a few weeks old. She was white with a perfect circle of brown hair on her side and a brown and black mask of hair on her head. She had a strip of white hair starting at her forehead that traveled down to her nose in the shape of a tornado. The black pigment on her nose was still filling in and in the shape of a heart. I had to admit, yes, she was very cute. He said that he inquired about the puppy and that she would be available to view in a couple of weeks, at the end of November, but the breeders would not allow her to be taken home until January.

I heaved a heavy sigh. Who was I kidding, he was going to do this whether I agreed or not. "Fine," I said, "but this is YOUR puppy. I'm not joking. I have enough on my plate." And in true Erik form he did his best nerdy rendition of the cabbage patch dance and of course I had to crack up.

And that was Erik. He was goofy and quick-witted and it endeared me to him.

One of our favorite things to do at Yucca Valley was sit on the front porch in the evenings. We were self-designated as "front-porch-sitters." After dinner he would grab a Coke from the refrigerator and I would pour a glass of red wine, and we would plop ourselves down in the large chairs that were nestled in the rocks right in front of our large picture window.

Our Yucca Valley house was situated on a small mountain and the street was a big horseshoe. It was like living on the side of a large bowl, or, more accurately, one of those manual orange juicing bowls. We would listen to the coyotes howling and conversing with each other in their unique language while we shared our day with each other. Taffy would be situated on my lap, alert to the surroundings, ready to bark at any rare passersby. In the spring, we welcomed the hummingbirds that came buzzing around. As the sun set further, the rabbits would come out of hiding and forage for food. It was quiet and it was peaceful. Maybe that's why Erik had such a hard time letting it go.

A few weeks passed and we were able to go see the puppy. It had been a long day for me but Erik really wanted to go that day so he could claim the one that he wanted.

As we entered the house, I told Erik, "This is all on you." I reminded him, "This is YOUR dog."

The woman that greeted us was a nice woman, friendly, someone you would expect to have the patience of dealing with a litter of puppies all day. As she greeted us and invited us into her home, we couldn't help but notice the adorable little puppy she was holding. "Oh, gosh, she is so cute!" I couldn't help myself. I was already getting sucked in.

"This one here is the runt." As the woman said that, Erik's ears perked up. Majesty had been the runt.

"Can I hold her?" he asked.

"Of course," she said as she handed the puppy over to him.

Clearly, he was conflicted now. This was not the puppy we had come to see.

As Erik and the woman made their way to the kitchen, I told them I was just going to have a seat on the floor near the puppies. I mean, I wasn't made of stone. What kind of person passes up an opportunity to hang out with puppies?

As soon as I sat down, while all the other puppies were running around and trying to figure out how to get around the boundaries that were set up, one little fluff ball marched right over my legs, climbed up the front of me, and planted little sweet kisses on the tip of my chin. It was the puppy we had come to see. I gathered her up in my arms and she scrambled to plant more kisses on my face. Finally, I held her little face up to mine and looked into her round dark eyes. My heart melted and my gut told me she would be ours. She had picked us.

When Erik came back to where I was, he tentatively inquired, "What do you think?"

"We're taking this one," I declared. Erik could tell by my voice that it was not open for debate.

Two months later we picked her up and she became part of our family. Erik chose the name Kira, which was Japanese for killer. He thought the name suited her. It was sweet and pretty on the surface, but it had the undertone of fierceness and bravery. And that was our Kira.

Just as Taffy had rejuvenated the puppy in Majesty, Kira was now doing the same for Taffy. It was fun to see them play together. We laughed as Kira would run underneath Taffy's legs, knowing she wouldn't be able to do that for long. She had a very sweet demeanor and she learned basic commands quickly. Within a week she was potty trained and sitting and staying.

To my relief, she was a nice distraction for both of us. We brought both Kira and Taffy to work every day with us and so Kira was extremely socialized. She adored Robin. If somebody new entered our office, her instinct to protect kicked in and she would bark out a warning, but as soon as she saw that we were okay with that person, then she deemed them acceptable to enter and would even allow them to give her a pet.

Corn Puffs

At the beginning of 2010, there was an annual local home show. Erik had registered and paid for it the year prior. Since there was no way to cancel the contract, he wanted to make the best of it. Who knows, he thought, maybe this could provide some solid leads of people who may have weathered the current financial storm and were looking to take advantage of desperate contractors. That was the hope anyway.

The morning of the first day he woke earlier than I had seen him wake in months. He wanted his booth to look perfect. He spent hours hauling in cabinets and countertops to the arena and setting up a mini kitchen in his 8x8 space. By the time he was finished, it looked beautiful. He felt certain he would attract many people to his booth. As we strolled the aisles of booths, we would stop and chat with other contractors who had the same idea. Some of the booths were extremely topnotch and enticing which signaled to us that they were just as desperate as we were. However, there were also obvious gaping holes where whoever had rented the space didn't even bother attending. Probably because they were already out of business.

When the show started, it was a much lower turnout than previous years, but that was not a surprise. About midway through the first day, I finished a deposition early and decided to visit Erik at his booth and see how he was doing. When I first approached, I saw that there were several couples in the booth engaging with Erik. My heart leapt with excitement, and I hung back until the people dispersed so as not to distract Erik. When Erik was then alone in the booth, I eagerly went up to him to see if there was any potential for business there. The disappointed expression on Erik's face was not what I was expecting. Unfortunately, those had been the only people all day that had stepped up to the booth and they weren't planning a remodel any time soon.

"But come here, I want to show you something," he said. He guided me across the aisle and a few booths down from his until we were standing in front of a table that was offering free samples of puffed rice and corn snacks that they were selling. They touted it as being like popcorn but without the kernels. "Try this," Erik said, and he handed me a small sample cup of the churro flavor. He awaited my opinion expectantly. "Oh, my gosh, this is so good!" I exclaimed.

Erik beamed. One of the women who was manning the booth came over and greeted Erik by name. Apparently, they had been introduced prior. Erik then introduced the woman to me.

"All day long I've watched her booth and she's been the busiest booth in the whole place."

"Wow, that's great," I said. *Oh, Lord, where is he going with this?*

We chatted with the woman about her company, and I got the distinct impression that they were both selling me on something. I was overcome with a feeling of dread. Nothing was broached in front of the woman, but as soon as we were alone, Erik began singing her accolades again and how well she was doing selling her product, how people weren't making big purchases but had no problem indulging in delicious snacks. *Oh, no, here it comes.*

"I think I could sell a ton of this stuff. We could go to all the different home shows, car shows, whatever, around the area and really clean up! And it could be fun!"

And there it was. Erik's next venture. I felt so torn between wanting to support Erik and his desire to do something to help, to contribute financially, and happy that he wasn't glued to the news, yet I was so apprehensive. Throughout the past 10 years together, I had learned something very important about Erik: He was an amazing visionist but not a great executor. For example, all the top-of-the-line workout equipment we needed for our exercise room because he was going to start working out; the '56 Chevy he was going to fix up; the Yucca Valley house that we were going to rent out; how he was going to market my business and also the salon, and he never followed up on any of those promises. I think at the time he committed

85

to them, he had every intention of doing it, he just got quickly distracted.

I tried to dissuade Erik, trying to get him to see the whole picture. It would take a lot of work and time traveling to all the different shows. Also, the expense of renting a booth space at these shows was not cheap. It would take a full day's worth of sales just to cover the booth fee. Not to mention the cost of the snacks themselves. How many bags of puffed corn and rice would need to be sold just to break even. But the next thing I know, we are visiting the facility where the sweet and salty snacks were manufactured, and we were discussing pricing with the woman from the booth.

I advised Erik, let's start out with what we need for one show, and then if we need more, we can buy more. But by the time we left, we had committed to purchasing $5,000 worth of product. The way Erik saw it, that $5,000 could easily yield us $15,000, giving us a net profit of $10,000. All we had to do was sell all of it.

God, thank you for Erik's optimism. Again, thank you for all that we're both learning from these difficult times and help me to be a supportive and loving wife to Erik.

Later that week the giant boxes of corn puffs were delivered to our warehouse and the following week Erik had his first show. I told Erik I would help him with the first one, but that with all the work I had, I wouldn't be able to commit to every weekend. He understood and was happy for my help.

When the weekend came for the show, we both got up early so that we could get the booth set up by the time the first show-goer walked by our booth. We started the weekend looking and sounding like Bill Mays, the outgoing spokesperson for OxyClean, dressed to impress and freshly showered, excited to engage people as they walked by. By Sunday afternoon we were more like a couple of carnies with disheveled clothes, my hair in a lazy ponytail, doing anything we could to get people's attention, calling out to passersby to come taste our product.

I'll hand it to the carnies, it's a successful tactic. We ended up with a busy booth and decent sales and our booth had a constant flow of customers, but the money earned didn't seem commensurate with the hours and labor involved. I was glad I had not committed to spending more weekends this way. Unfortunately, Erik was also disenchanted with the whole proposition and so that was the last show that either of us did.

When we finally had to let go of the office building, we also left the giant boxes of corn puff snacks. As we drove away from the warehouse for the last time, I couldn't help but chuckle at the thought of someone discovering the unexpected contents of those boxes. Now it is reminder of Erik's unwavering optimism, even in the face of challenges, and the lessons we learned along the way.

Denver

In the spring of 2010, I had been in a long grueling deposition all day and traffic had been a beast. By the time I made it home, it was late and I was tired. I poured myself a glass of wine and perused the fridge for any leftovers I could eat quickly and easily. I was happy to find some pizza from the night before.

As I sat at the kitchen table with my wine and pizza, allowing myself a relaxing long exhale, Erik came into the room, grabbed a Coke, and sat with me.

"Honey, why don't you drink some water?" I asked, knowing what the answer would be but feeling like I had to try again.

"I'm doing good today; this is only my fourth one."

It was a losing battle, trying to convince him to give up Coke.

As he sat down, I could tell that something was on his mind. I couldn't help but think, *now what?* Erik finally said, "I've been thinking." *Oh, no. Whenever he says that, it's not good.*

"What do you think about moving to Denver?"

I sat there for about 30 seconds. I knew he chose Denver not just for the beautiful mountains but also because his brother lived there. Erik and I had been to Denver several times throughout the years, and I enjoyed the clear blue sky and scenic mountains. And that was all I needed to think about. I looked at my watch and said, "I can be ready in 10 minutes."

The truth was, California had chewed us up and spit us out. In addition to the obvious, it was also the cost of living, the taxes, the smog, and the traffic. The traffic! I felt like I spent my 30s sitting in a car. In fact, for the past year and a half, I started using the carpool lane by myself. I calculated that it saved me almost an hour every morning and evening. That cut my total commute time from five hours a day to three hours a day. That was significant. After a while, the threat of being caught and being cited for $350 didn't bother me. I used to joke that I was going to have a check already written out, and when the officer stopped me, I would gladly hand him the check and say, "Here you go!" with a smile on my face, feeling justified that the amount of time that I saved had been totally worth it.

And so when Erik mentioned Denver, it felt like I was being thrown a life line.

Erik said, "The only thing I'm hesitant about is not living near water. I've always lived near the ocean."

"How often do we go to the beach?" I asked. It was easy to quantify because it was almost never. Maybe once or twice a year? We had neither the time nor desire to sit in traffic and search for parking.

"Yeah, that's true."

Of course, we couldn't just pick up and move. We had responsibilities we had to take care of. The mortgage company for the Yucca Valley home had been unbudging to work with us and so concluded that we would need to let it go. They offered a $2,000 incentive if we moved out by May 1st. I had been hearing of people who were so angry about being foreclosed on that they were pouring cement down their drains, trashing the house, and taking everything that wasn't nailed down to the floor, including every light bulb and fixture. I figured I might have a little leverage.

"How about you give us $5,000 and we will move out by June 1st."

"I'm sorry, I don't think we can do that," was the response from the representative.

"My husband spent months laying a travertine floor throughout the whole house. We'll take it with us if we have to."

"$5,000 and June 1st should be fine."

It was piddly compared to what we were losing but it felt good to have a slight win for once.

By June 1st we weren't ready to move to Denver yet and so we moved into our office condo in San Bernardino. In the upstairs we had a conference room we turned into a bedroom. Erik had already added a bathroom and shower in the warehouse. It wasn't ideal, but it was comfortable. Plus, you couldn't beat the commute! Robin used to joke that if we ever came downstairs in pajamas, she would quit. Needless to say, that never happened.

Thank you, God, for this space and a place to stay. Thank you for always providing for our needs.

For the rest of the summer, we stayed there while we plotted our get-away. I really wasn't interested in running the agency anymore. Truth be told, it was really Robin who ran it anyway. All I did was run payroll twice a month. My first inclination was to just shut it down. I still had a few faithful clients but they didn't produce enough income to substantiate keeping the agency. One day I threw the idea out to Robin if she would want to purchase the agency. After some negotiations we came to a fair price and she took full control of the agency in the fall. What a relief off my shoulders.

Thank you, God, for blessing me with the gift that Robin has been to me. In so many ways. Please bless her with success and prosperity.

Saying goodbye to all of our family there was the final and most difficult thing we had to do before leaving California. I had been so blessed in California with my Aunt Kay but also my Aunt Margaret, my mother's younger sister, and numerous cousins from my mother's siblings. Saying goodbye was reminiscent of when I left Minnesota and when I left New York, the bittersweet pain of leaving friends and family behind, yet knowing without hesitation that is what needs to happen next. It's a consoling feeling but it doesn't make it less painful.

When we moved to Denver, Westminster to be exact, we moved in with Marshall, Erik's brother. I easily found work in downtown Denver and so most of my days were busy. Erik found ways to keep busy as well. First, he cleared out Marshall's overgrown and neglected backyard. Next, he built a multi-level deck that any decking contractor would have been impressed with. It was beautiful. Marshall's backyard went from a jungle of weeds to an inviting and comfortable space to relax. More noticeably, Erik was able to take pride in something again. Despite the fact that he wasn't working and he had no prospects, he seemed content and happy.

In 2011 Erik found a job with Sears, doing estimates and sales for their housing division. It was a commissioned base job and it required tons of traveling all over Colorado and into Wyoming. The job description sounded like a perfect fit for Erik but I knew he was just taking it out of obligation to contribute. I appreciated that, but all the nights that he spent on the road unraveled me. For months I spent many evenings sitting up, worrying, waiting. He would call me from the road, trying to navigate through snow storms and icy roads. To add insult to injury, the economy was still in recovery mode and sales were few and far between. He stuck it out for almost a year but we finally had to accept that the pay he was receiving was not worth all the time he was spending and the wear and tear on his truck.

In May of 2012 we had another move, this time only a few blocks away. We enjoyed the time with Marshall but we felt ready to have our own place again. We rented a cozy little house with a fenced backyard, perfect for the dogs. It even had a doggy door, which we were new to, but instantly fell in love with, and so did the dogs, enjoying the freedom of going out whenever they wanted. Especially Kira and especially in the winter. She would plop herself down in a snowbank and would stay there all day long. Every now and then she would be curious as to what we were doing and so she would stick her head through the doggy door and just look at us, confirm she wasn't missing anything, and return to her snow pile.

Taffy was more content to stay indoors and out of the weather. His graying face was a reminder that he was climbing up in age but I hated to think of that. I couldn't forget what had popped into my mind that day at the mall all those years ago in Minnesota when we first claimed each other. 15 *years*. Taffy wouldn't be 15 until May of 2013 and I felt confident that we had at least that much time together. However, by October of 2012 I couldn't deny the fact that Taffy was suffering.

Taffy had an infatuation with Q-tips. I have no explanation for it. And he wasn't one of those dogs that would eat anything and everything you put in front of him. He didn't eat socks or rocks or anything else that was nonedible, just those darn Q-tips. He would pull them out of the bathroom trash. Erik cleaned his ears practically every day and so there was no shortage. I tried to get Erik to close the bathroom door but he often forgot. We could always tell when Taffy had gotten into them because he would poop out perfect bundles of the plastic and cotton spears. They didn't even appear to be chewed.

The decline of Taffy's health, however, started with his legs. He was able to walk but the stairs had become difficult. Ever since Taffy came into my life, he followed me wherever I went. I couldn't go to the bathroom without him poking his head in to check on me. One of my favorite ways to decompress throughout the years had been taking Taffy for walks. He required no leash, he would just trot happily in front of me, his tail lifted high. Every few minutes he would turn around to make sure I was still with him, and he would slow down if I was too far behind, and I swear he would smile at me. No matter what was happening that day, Taffy could put a smile on my face and remind me what was important. Is there anything better than a happy dog?

It was the saddest feeling the day when I climbed the five stairs in our house leading to the office and Taffy just stared at me from the bottom of the steps, devastated that he couldn't follow, and so I began carrying him up and down the stairs with me. His 40-pound frame filled up my arms just like his love filled my heart.

Taffy also started losing his eyesight and his hearing. It became most apparent one day when I was walking him and we came by a house with a stone turtle on the lawn. It attracted Taffy's attention, and he engaged in a stare-down until he deemed the cement turtle was not a threat.

Further up the street, as we walked, there was a tall wooden fence that abutted right up next to the sidewalk. As we walked the length of the fence, the dog on the other side caught our scent and charged the fence. I couldn't see the dog but it was easy to guess it was a big dog by the ferociousness of its bark. By the time we neared the end of the fence, there was no mistaking the dog was just a fence board away from devouring us, and Taffy just stopped, lifted his head, and pulled his ears back as if to say, "Do you hear something?"

All of that continued for several months, but then in October he started vomiting and not eating. My guess was that he finally got a Q-tip lodged somewhere that wasn't conducive to ear-cleaning devices. This is the day every good dog-owner dreads. In so many ways dogs become our children but they are not children. It's a dichotomy that is hard to delineate in our hearts. When one or the other gets sick, however, you weigh the options completely different. When it's your child that becomes ill, there is no question, you bring them right away to the doctor or to the hospital. When it's your pet, you have so many other considerations. The biggest one, in my opinion, is the age of them. For a dog of Taffy's size, 15 years would have been pushing it. He was 14-1/2. And the next consideration, if I'm being honest, is cost. How much are we willing to spend to fix a dog that will likely not be able to walk in a few months. When all things were considered, we felt like the humane thing to do was to put him down.

Ever since my dad and I had to put Benji down, my childhood dog, I swore I would never do it again. But in this instance it felt necessary and compassionate. Taffy had had a good life. He had been loved and spoiled just like dogs should be.

I was able to schedule a home visit so that Taffy didn't have the trauma of being on a cold exam table in a sterile environment. I wanted for Taffy what I wanted for me and anyone I loved, to just die peacefully in bed.

When the veterinarian came to our house, he advised that we put Kira outside during the procedure and then to let her in afterwards so that she could understand what happened. Erik and I agreed.

We then went over to Taffy's bed. The fact that Taffy hadn't risen or barked or acknowledged somebody coming into our house was just further confirmation that we were doing the right thing. The vet, according to protocol, needed to do a short exam on Taffy to make sure the procedure was warranted. After studying his gums and tongue, he confirmed that Taffy wasn't doing well, and even if we didn't do this, he wouldn't last long. It was comforting to know we made the right decision, yet my heart was breaking at the thought of a world without my Taffy.

As I knelt on the floor next to Taffy, I wrapped my arms around him and lowered my face right next to his ear. "You're a good boy, Taffy. I love you so much. You've been such a good boy." I repeated that over and over, my eyes flooded with tears, until the procedure was over. Taffy hadn't struggled one bit, but I could feel it when he was gone. Yet I couldn't let go. I felt like part of me went with him. The world just seemed to lose its color without Taffy in it. I buried my face in his fur and I sobbed the tears that only someone else that has gone through this experience knows. It was visceral and true agony to say goodbye to such a loyal and loving friend.

Finally, when I had no more sobs, Erik helped me up and we embraced, consoling each other. Then we let Kira in so that she would understand why Taffy would no longer be with us. When we opened the door, however, she was more excited by the vet and the new smells of him and all his equipment, she didn't even go over to Taffy. We gave her several minutes, but she just wasn't curious. The vet suggested that we put Kira back outside while he took Taffy out of the house. Kira's size and breed was very intimidating, and the vet said it wasn't uncommon for the remaining dogs to become protective of the deceased dog and not allow them to be taken, even biting or attacking the person attempting to do so. Erik put Kira back outside while I said one more goodbye to Taffy and watched as the vet very gently carried Taffy out to his vehicle and drove away.

Kira was very anxious to come back inside and so we once again opened the door. First, she ran right over to where Taffy had been lying on his bed. She sniffed all around and then darted up the stairs and went into each bedroom, then the bathroom. Next, she went downstairs and did the same thing. It was excruciating to watch her look for her friend and big brother. What was she thinking, I wondered. Did she understand death? Taffy had left the house without her before and she had never searched like this. Eventually she gave up the search, but instead of retreating outside, where she spent most of her time, she chose to stay inside with us, sitting next to our chairs as we watched TV, in the same spot Taffy used to. Somehow she figured it out. She understood. And our lives went on.

Starting over in St. Louis

In the spring of 2013, Erik Googled "What the hell does an out of work contractor do?"

Low and behold, insurance adjusting popped up first on the list. Intrigued, Erik clicked on the first link and read about what insurance adjusting entails and he felt a twinge of excitement.

"Adjusters inspect property damage or personal injury claims to determine how much the insurance company should pay for the loss."

Erik immediately began researching the steps to becoming an adjuster and what the requirements were. It turned out there was a class beginning the following month, in April. We both agreed that this could be a new beginning for him.

Thank you, God, for showing this to Erik, for guiding us to this place at this time.

After a few days of classes, Erik began speaking of a friend he had made named David. David was from St. Louis, Missouri, and was attending the class because he was working for a roofer in St. Louis. St. Louis at that time was in the pathway of fierce and frequent hail storms, causing damage over and over again to any homes that happened to be in the way. The roofers were being severely delayed because there simply were not enough insurance adjusters to inspect the roofs of the houses. David concluded that this would be a good opportunity to get out of the roofing trade and start a new career.

Erik and Dave hit it off immediately. As the class progressed, they started to form a plan of working together as public insurance adjusters. Public adjusters didn't work for insurance companies, they were hired by homeowners to ensure that they received all that they were entitled to under the terms of their policy. This spoke directly to Erik's heart. He wanted to protect people from unethical insurance companies. Since most people are not aware of the exact terms of their homeowner's policy, many insurance companies will take advantage of that.

Once again, I came home from work to see a familiar look on Erik's face. *Here we go. Buckle up.*

"So, you know, Dave says there is a ton of work in St. Louis so I've been thinking of how I can commute."

"Commute to St. Louis?" That sounded absurd to me. It was a 12-hour drive. Then I realized that he just didn't have the heart to ask me to move again.

"If you're going to be spending so much time there, why don't we explore the option of moving there. Let's go check it out."

I wasn't in love with the idea of moving again, especially because we had nobody there. At least in Denver we had some family, and for the first time in years I had the time to develop a new friendship. But on the other hand, Erik had a new opportunity to do something he could enjoy and be successful at. In fairness to Erik, I had to consider that. My profession allowed me to work anywhere close to a big city.

Within weeks we were standing in downtown St. Louis. It was a beautiful spring day. I interviewed with two prospective court reporting agencies and felt confident I could do the same work and receive similar pay to what I was accustomed to. I couldn't find a reason not to move there.

God, thank you so much for this opportunity. Your love and mercy astound me.

During the following month I finished up all the outstanding transcripts I had, began packing again, and searching CraigsList and other websites for house rentals in the St. Louis area. We needed a house with a backyard for Kira.

When Erik and I had moved into the house in Westminster, we both knew it was temporary and that we wanted to eventually buy another house someday. The thought was a little scary for me but I knew we had to get back on the horse. We would be smarter this time. So, for the first time ever, I felt called to do a weekly fast as I prayed for where we would live next. I had absolutely no idea where it would be, what it would be, but in my mind I assumed it would be in Denver or the surrounding area. I felt that the next move was going to be significant somehow and so I wanted to make sure it was exactly where God wanted us. Every Wednesday for that whole year I would rise early and go to the office where I had my journal and Bible and several devotional books. I allowed myself coffee in the morning and water throughout the day but I abstained from food until dinner time. My fasts were from 6 p.m. Tuesday to 6 p.m. the following night.

I would spend those mornings in prayer, meditation, and journaling my thoughts and feelings of where I wanted to live. But most of all, I wanted to live where God wanted us to live and so that was the basic theme of my fasting. What I had never considered was that God had another city and state in mind. Why do I always forget that God's blessings know no bounds! Even with the hesitancy to leave family and friends again, it felt right, and I trusted God.

After scouring the different websites and conferring with David on which areas of St. Louis were the safest, I found a house in Webster Groves. We would be renting it just based off pictures and so we had to feel confident that at least the area was safe and known for well-kept houses, and then cross our fingers that the pictures were sincere depictions of the space.

God, thank you so much for this house and for guiding us to St. Louis. Lord, can you please show us somehow that this is your will for Erik and me.

Suddenly, *lilacs* popped into my head, my favorite scent.

It's impossible for me to pass a lilac bush without plunging my nose into the deep purple flowers and inhaling as though it were my last breath. If you Google what lilacs smell like, it will tell you it's fresh, spring-like, perfumery, perhaps a cross between lavender and wild berries. To me, it smells like the carefree days of my youth and the sweet anticipation of summertime.

The house I grew up in had three entrances: the front door, which only salespeople and people we didn't know went to; the back door that went to the screened-in patio and out to the back yard which we used to go to the garage or carport; and then the side door. Our next-door neighbors' lilac bush was right on the border of our two properties and located right outside our side door to the house. In the summertime, this was the main door we used. It's where we parked our bikes and friends came knocking. For the three or four weeks that the lilacs were blooming, you couldn't leave or enter the side door without the sweet fragrance filling up your nose.

The summers of my generation were a magical time, and the fragrance of lilacs signaled the beginning of it. The beginning of lemonade stands and splashing through the sprinkler, running around barefoot and cartwheels on the grass. We spent hours just sitting in the front yard, studying worms and playing with rollie pollies. There were no playdates; you played with whoever lived on your street, usually with very little supervision. The only water we drank was either from a hose or mixed with colored powder and a cup of sugar. We were shown how to look both ways before crossing the street and then trusted to do it on our own. When we fell and scraped a knee, mom doused it with hydrogen peroxide, slapped a Band-Aid on it, and sent us back out to play. We were free to explore and climb trees and we rode bikes without helmets and no hands on the handlebars. It was pure magic.

Okay, God, if the house has a lilac bush, I'll know it's from you. And then I kind of chuckled to myself on that last prayer. I felt like it was an easy lob for God since that part of the country had lilac bushes practically in front of every house, but whatever.

We arrived to St. Louis on the Sunday night of Memorial Day weekend, 2013. Erik had made one trip already and brought

99

a load of furniture and so we had a bed set up for us when we arrived. I was grateful because it was late when we rolled into St. Louis, nearly 2:00 in the morning. And it was dark due to the lack of a moon that night. Dark like you can't see your hand in front of your face. We parked on the driveway next to the house, near the back door. Any light that the streetlights provided was blocked by the house and so it was good that Erik knew the way to get to the door. Just as we approached the house, in the cool summer night, my nose was filled with the aroma of lilacs, as if the bush was right in our faces but we just couldn't see it because of the dark.

"Mmmmmm, Erik, do you smell that? It smells amazing."

"Huh? Oh, yeah, lilacs. They smell good. Now, come on, I want to get to bed. I'm tired."

I smiled a big smile and gave a nod to God before going into the house. Whether it was God or not that there happened to be a lilac bush there, it didn't matter. I'd give God the win.

The next morning, however, after getting dressed and exploring the house, I went out the back door to greet my lilacs. I walked down the steps and looked all around. Not a single lilac to be seen. Not in my yard, nor in our neighbor's yard. Now I really had to chuckle, then laugh, and then cry. Isn't it just like me to put Him in a box and isn't it just like God to come up with the unimaginable. And that's the benefit of trusting God with our problems and our future. We are so limited in what we see as possible outcomes, but with God there are no limits! All we have to say is, God, I give this over to you. Your will be done.

God, you never cease to amaze me. Thank you for doing only what you can do. Thank you for this house in this neighborhood in this city in this state. I have no doubt that we are exactly where you want us to be.

Later that morning, some of our new neighbors stopped by and invited us to attend the block party that was happening on our street later in the afternoon. After several hours of unpacking, we began to hear chatter coming from outside. As we stepped out the front door, I felt like I had stepped back in time to my childhood. The houses along the street adorned American flags proudly. We noticed the street had been blocked from traffic and people were starting to prepare for the festivities. Young mothers were setting up tables and chairs while the fathers wheeled their grills out onto the street, one lined up next to the other. Kids that ran the age gamut ran in and around the street, chasing each other, playing catch, riding scooters and laughing. Mothers and fathers yelled out cautions and reminders of good manners. As more and more people joined, young and old, everyone was greeted with smiles and hugs. As we made our way to the street, we were quickly welcomed and introduced to the rest of our neighbors. A feeling of belonging and contentment spread over me that I hadn't felt for a very long time. There was no doubt we were exactly where we were supposed to be.

Not long after moving in, Erik and I were sitting on the front porch of our newly rented house. He was enjoying a Coke and I had a fresh glass of sauvignon blanc, and we were watching the fireflies dance around our front yard, something I hadn't experienced since living in Minnesota. Feelings of nostalgia always engulf me at the sight of fireflies, reminding me of the carefree days my childhood. Kira was perched with her head resting on the railing, watching them with us. Out of nowhere Erik said, "I'm really glad that God brought us here. Our lives are so much better than they were in California."

My eyes filled with tears and my heart swelled with gratitude. Erik finally understood the power of trusting God, and for the first time since I met him, he was content. And me?

I realized that the illusion of "home" that I had been searching for was with me all along. Home was wherever Erik was.

It had been a long journey, but in the end, we traded a million dollars of equity for a strengthened love and respect for each other and Erik's newfound trust and faith in God. I don't believe it was God's fault for us losing everything in California. That was ours. But what God did with it is what matters. And for that, I will always be grateful.

God, it has been a long and often bumpy ride to where we are now, but I thank you for every inch of our journey. It was worth the wait.

CHAPTER 5

Stay In The Present

When your hourglass is flipped and the sand begins to descend, you immediately start looking at the calendar. Three months to a year covers a lot of territory. I was diagnosed in June. I started wondering, will I make it to my next birthday in September? How about Thanksgiving? Christmas? And if I do make it, what condition will I be in? As I enjoyed the warm summer days, I would think, *will this be my last summer? Will this be my last 4th of July fireworks?*

Such thoughts, though natural, are as futile as trying to add grains to an empty hourglass. Whenever those thoughts popped up, I tried to quickly push them aside and remind myself that no one knows their expiration date. Of all people who had a reason to worry about their future it is Jesus. Jesus *knew* his destiny and he *knew* that worrying about it would not make a difference, and so he doesn't want us to.

In Matthew 6:27 Jesus admonishes us: "Can any one of you by worrying add a single hour to your life?"

And the answer is, of course not. Yet we eagerly take on that needless suffering.

Jesus goes on to say, in Matthew 6:34: "Therefore do not worry about tomorrow, for tomorrow will worry about itself. Each day has enough trouble of its own."

For some reason, when I picture him saying this, at the end I can imagine him giving a little grin, maybe a wink. I don't think he was saying every day you will have trouble, I feel like maybe he was teasing a bit. I love how thorough Matthew is as he recites Jesus's words, but what I think is missed sometimes is the manner in which it's spoken. I have no doubt that Jesus had a sense of humor and I can envision His audience responding with a chuckle.

I wish I could say that when I read this in the Bible I decided to live my life that way. Like when I read about Corrie Ten Boom's lice. Unfortunately, it took a tragedy for me to put this into practice. It became a practice borne out of necessity. I quickly learned that when your future is ripped out from underneath you, you have nowhere to reside but the present. It's a daunting existence at first when you're not used to it, focusing on today only, not looking ahead, and giving your unknown future completely and entirely over to God. It takes total trust and, sometimes, desperation.

The Day Everything Happened

June 2014: *I wonder if I should have pushed Erik harder to go to the ER.* I heard his voice in my head replaying the statement he had made just an hour prior. "There was some blood in the toilet. It looked like a lot. Or maybe not. Maybe the water just made it look like a lot."

It had sounded like he was trying to convince himself more than me.

I should have insisted. There was a hospital right there.

Instead, we were driving down I-15 towards Las Vegas from southern California. We had spent a week there visiting family and now we were heading home. I was driving a rental car but Erik was in a Chevy Tahoe in front of me, which we had purchased that morning. The plan was to drop off the rental car and then drive together back to Missouri after stopping in Denver to pick up Kira from Marshall's.

I'm sure he's fine. He's had blood in his stool before. He's always been okay.

From the time I met Erik he had stomach issues. He was never officially diagnosed but I think he possibly had Crohn's Disease or Celiac Disease. He was in a constant state of diarrhea or constipation. He was often bloated after eating and could also have stomach pain. He was able to keep it under control if he avoided foods with gluten, but since we were on the last day of our vacation, he had decided to forego feeling good for his favorite sandwich.

He said he felt okay.

When we left the restaurant in Riverside after having lunch with his best friend, JR, I let him talk me into driving to Victorville before deciding if he should go to the hospital. "We have to stop there for gas and there's a hospital there. If I don't feel better, we'll go to the ER there."

About 30 minutes later, after pulling up to the gas pumps in Victorville, I got out of the car and approached Erik where he was fueling the Tahoe. "How are you feeling?" I asked him.

Erik thoughtfully rubbed his hand over his bloated belly as if his hand would be able to detect any threat.

"I think I'm okay. I really want to get to Vegas and get the car returned. And if I don't feel well, I can go to the ER there."

I warned him, "Are you sure? Vegas is three hours away and there's nothing in between."

He again waved his magic hand over his stomach. "I'll be fine."

In all honesty, I believed him. I trusted his judgement. He was not a careless person. He also wasn't one of those macho guys who would refuse to go to the hospital even if he had a limb dangling off him. He had assessed how he felt and I trusted that he was making the correct judgment call. I had no idea at that moment how many times I would replay that exchange in my head.

For that next hour as we drove through the brown and boring desert, I allowed my mind to wander, resolved that Erik was going to be fine. After all, this wasn't exactly a new development. He often felt horrible after he ate, especially anything with bread. In an effort to distract myself from distressing thoughts, I started to think about the wonderful time we had just had in California. The previous Sunday came to mind, the condo we rented near Mission Beach, where Tosha and her husband Kevin, his Aunt Nancy and all his cousins and their children came for the day and we all enjoyed a beautiful day on the beach, swimming and paddle-boarding. Since Tosha and Kevin were soon being transferred to Italy, and Erik and I now living in St. Louis, it made our time together that much more treasured and appreciated, not knowing when the next time would be that we would all be together.

Then I heard Erik's voice again, "It looked like a lot of blood." *Dang it, what if he's wrong about being okay. But he really thought about it. No, I'm sure he's okay.* As much as I tried to convince myself that this was no different than all the previous times he hadn't felt well after eating, I couldn't shake the feeling that something didn't feel right.

15 minutes from State Line (now known as Primm), Erik was calling my cell phone. I picked up quickly. "How are you doing on gas?" he asked.

"I'm fine," I said, "don't worry about that. How are you feeling?"

"Not very good. I'm getting a pretty sharp pain about every 10 minutes, like clockwork."

"Okay. We're not returning the rental car first, we're going straight to the ER."

"Yeah, that's probably a good idea." And just before he hung up, I heard him yawn.

I don't know why that stuck out to me or why I remember that he yawned. Maybe because that's another conversation that would run in a loop through my head for months to come.

At some point when I was young, whenever I felt fearful of something, I would imagine the worst possible outcome. It seemed like a secret power to keep really horrible things from happening. If I would just imagine something really awful happening, that would keep it from happening. It was kind of a gut reaction for me now, something I did automatically. And so my mind conjured up the worst possible outcome, Erik dies. The minute my mind went there, I had to reel it in. I instantly felt a lump in my throat and tears forming in my eyes. *Nope, we're not going there. We'll get to the hospital and Erik is going to be okay.*

Five minutes later, I saw that Erik was signaling to move over a lane, then another lane, and I could see he was planning to pull over to the side of the road. *Poor guy, he has diarrhea and he can't hold it any longer.* I noticed there wasn't much around to shield him from view. *He must really have to go.* Again, not the first time he's had to pull over. In fact, on the road up to Lake Arrowhead, off the main road, there is a corner where Erik had to pull over and make like a bear in the woods. Tyler had been with him, and Erik was able to make a joke of it, forever labeling that curve "crap corner."

We pulled off safely to the side and we were seconds away from being at a complete stop. I stopped and put the car in park, but I saw Erik was still inching forward, but suddenly the

Tahoe took a sharp right turn into the desert. He wasn't going fast but he wasn't stopping. I stared in disbelief as the Tahoe bounced over sand dunes and tumbleweeds, through a barbed wire fence. It finally came to a stop about 50 yards away when it hit a crevice with the left tires and it rolled onto the driver's side, the roof, and then back onto the driver's side.

I was unable to form a thought in my head. I was shaking uncontrollably, and I couldn't breathe. I didn't know what to do first: Call 911? Try to go to him to see if he was okay? I grabbed my phone to call 911. However, I couldn't remember how to unlock the screen and my hands were trembling so much I couldn't even work the phone.

Suddenly I knew I had to go to him but I had taken my shoes off for the drive. I couldn't go out in the desert without shoes. *Where the hell are my shoes?* Once I had them, I wrestled with getting them on. *Why did I wear these damn shoes?* They had a separate loop for the big toe and I struggled putting them on ordinarily. Now I was trying to do so with shaking hands. It was as though my mind and my hands weren't connected anymore. I couldn't get them to work fast enough.

I finally got my shoes on and tried to exit the rental car. *How do I unlock the doors?* As I shook, I looked all over for the unlock button. This just escalated my breathing. *This damn rental car! Get me out of this car!* It began to feel like I was trapped in the car underwater and it was quickly filling up.

I finally got out and noticed another car had stopped. A young couple were walking towards me. I was never happier to see two people I didn't know. They appeared to be in their mid to late 30s. She was athletic looking with long dark hair and dressed in jean shorts and a T-shirt. He was a bit taller than she was, dressed in jeans and polo shirt with light brown hair. As they walked towards me, I felt like I might pass out. I just couldn't breathe. I was just sucking in air but nothing was coming out. *This isn't happening. This isn't happening. This isn't happening. This isn't happening.* I said that as many times as it took for me to gain control of my breathing again. And as I stood in the desert and waited for help to come, I just kept reciting that over and over again. Then I told myself, *until someone tells me otherwise, he is fine. He is okay.*

I went from hyperventilating and panicking to feeling absolutely nothing.

As the husband/boyfriend went to use the emergency phone on the side of the highway, the wife/girlfriend and I started across the desert to get to where the Tahoe was resting. If I ever did learn their names, I have no memory.

Wife/Girlfriend got to Erik first. It was slightly rough terrain and you had to get over a mangled barbed wire fence. She was wearing tennis shoes and I had flimsy sandals on. Looking back, I don't think I wanted to get there first. Even though I was telling myself that he was fine, somehow I knew he wasn't. I was afraid to see anything that I knew I couldn't "unsee."

The Tahoe was resting on the driver's side and it was also in a crevice, and so the passenger side of the truck was at the level of her shoulders. By standing on her toes, she was able to peer into the front passenger window. I stopped moving closer when I saw that she was there. "Can you see him?"

"I can. It's hard to tell but I think I saw him breathe." The way she said it, I knew it was said for my benefit.

I made my way closer as fast as I could, barely feeling all the rocks and pebbles between my feet and the soles of my sandals. The wind was ferocious and blew my hair into my face, making it difficult at times to see where I was stepping. I finally arrived at her location next to the window. *Do I want to see this? I have to see for myself.* I stood on my toes and looked down into the window. I could see that Erik had been ejected from the Tahoe since he was pinned beneath the Tahoe. *He must have taken his seat belt off because of the pains he had been feeling.* As I peered through the passenger window, down through the interior of the vehicle, and through the driver window, the only view was of Erik on his back. I could see his chin was turned to one side and his arm was resting on his stomach. *He looks like he's asleep.* I had seen Erik many times in that exact same position; however, it was usually on a sofa or recliner with golf or football on TV.

I backed away from the Tahoe. Wife/Girlfriend said, "We should probably move away from the car in case gasoline is leaking." I moved away, not because of the potential threat, but because I knew Erik was gone. I knew but I didn't want to know. I was not ready for that yet. And so I kept the fairytale going, that Erik was okay until somebody told me otherwise.

We made our way back across the desert and to the side of the road. Husband/Boyfriend had returned and said he was able to get in touch with emergency services and they were on their way, but because of the remote location, it could take a little while.

In the meantime, I stood in the desert like a statue. My hair whipped around my face and sand and dust pelted my legs. *Erik, are you here right now? Are you floating above me, looking down, wondering what's wrong with me, why I'm not crying? I'm sorry. Please don't think that I don't love you. Why didn't you listen to me? Why didn't you go to the ER?* Somehow, as I stood there in the vast lonely desert, I didn't feel alone. I could feel God's arms around me and His heart breaking for me. It comforted me.

As the time passed, I felt like I was watching myself in a movie, like it wasn't real, and that I wasn't being as dramatic as Hollywood would depict this scene. If this were a movie, I imagined my character would be on the ground, inconsolable, wailing and carrying on. It occurs to me how we allow movies and TV dictate how we should act, how we would expect ourselves to act, in different situations. And if we don't act in accordance with that expectation, we feel like we're doing it wrong, having the wrong reaction. I've now learned that there is no wrong reaction. I've also learned not to judge others' reactions. Because until it happens to you, you have no idea how you will respond.

Eventually a police officer arrived and then a firetruck and ambulance. While the firefighters attempted to retrieve Erik and the Tahoe, I sat in the back of the police car, explaining to the police officer what happened. I sat there numb, dreading the moment I knew was coming, yet still not allowing myself to believe it. The police officer sat in the front while he asked me questions. If I had to guess, he was in his late 30s, white, bald, either by choice or by genetics, hard to tell. He didn't appear to be very tall and had a broad chest. And he was kind. I could tell by the way he was asking me questions, he felt compassion for me. I wondered if he wondered why I wasn't crying. I wondered if everybody wondered that. I knew how cold-hearted I must appear.

After we finished the interview, he got out and came over to my open back seat door and stood next to me. As he was standing there, another officer came up to him. He said to the officer who had interviewed me, "The coroner should be here in about 10 minutes."

I looked at the face of the officer that interviewed me. His eyes shot daggers at the other officer. He was clearly not happy that he said this in front of me. The time had come. I had to ask, "Are you telling me my husband is dead?"

I don't remember the response or who responded, if there was any response at all. I just know I crumpled in the back seat of the police car. I fell to the side and buried my face in my hands as I lay across the back seat. Never in my life have I cried such a painful cry. As I watched my future of growing old with Erik being wiped clean like a dry erase board, the sobs were loud and uncontrollable. I couldn't cry hard enough. My chest felt like it couldn't contain that much heartache at one time. I thought of Erik's kids, his brother, who had just found out he was going to be a father for the first time, how excited Erik was about being an uncle. Over and over I thought, *how can your life change so quickly? I just don't understand, I had just spoken to him. How can he be gone?*

I have no idea how long I cried for. It could have been 3 minutes or 30 minutes. Time seemed as irrelevant as the future I had planned with Erik.

When I thought I had composed myself, I sat up straight on the seat again and I called my sister, my person. She was always my first phone call when my life took a turn I wasn't expecting or wanting. She picked up on the second ring, like she always does. I could barely get the words out and the sobbing escaped again. All I remember is she vowed to be on the next flight.

I tried again to compose myself and I somehow managed to call Tosha and Marshall. Tosha and Kevin volunteered to call Tyler, and Marshall said he and his wife Mandy would be on the soonest flight they could get.

Finally, I was able to take a breath, the tears slowed down, and I went into a state of numbness. I was seeing and hearing but feeling nothing. I learned that a tow truck would be taking my rental car back to Enterprise. I guess once they heard the circumstances, they were happy to take care of the arrangements.

The kind police officer asked if he could call anyone to come pick me up. I stared at him and considered who I would call. Anybody that would come was at least 3 hours away. I decided to catch a ride on the tow truck to Las Vegas and have them drop me off at a hotel that Erik and I used to stay at. It was on the outskirts of Vegas and nowhere near the strip or the craziness. It was clean and updated and reasonably priced and familiar to me. It made sense. Marshall and Mandy would fly into Vegas that night and stay with me. My sister couldn't get a flight until the following morning, arriving at 8 a.m.

I asked the police officer if the emergency workers could retrieve my suitcase from the Tahoe. I had nothing with me but my purse. Everything was in the suitcase. They made a diligent attempt but the suitcase had landed someplace they weren't able to get to yet. I didn't care.

I climbed up into the tow truck and sat beside a kind younger gentleman who was looking at me very compassionately and a little apprehensively, perhaps secretly hoping I would not have a total breakdown on the way. But I just sat there as we made the 45-minute drive, thinking nothing, feeling nothing. I did what came natural, I asked the tow truck driver about his life, did he have kids, small talk. When we arrived to the hotel, he asked me gently, "Are you sure you're going to be okay?"

I have no idea but what other choice do I have? "I'll be fine. Thank you though. Thanks for the ride." I must have sounded somewhat convincing because the next thing I know he's gone and I'm standing in front of the receptionist, checking into my room.

"Hello and welcome to South Point. And how are you today?"

Do I really answer that?

"I'm fine."

We finish the check-in as I look around. I see the table where Erik and I sat and played 3-card poker one night. That was after we had seen Phantom of the Opera. The casino in the hotel was busy and there was a good energy among the tables. I can see Erik seated in front of the dealer, me standing behind him, observing and collecting any winnings, our usual habit. It was towards the end of the night and it was quieting down. We happened to be the only players at the table. Erik often liked to chat with dealers if they appeared friendly. That night it was an older woman with big hair and easy smile. "So how about a straight flush?" Erik joked. That was the hand with the highest payout.

"Actually, I'm due for one," she replied with a grin.

"Tell you what, you deal me a straight flush, I'll split it with you." We all chuckled knowing the odds of that happening were extremely slim. And then to our amaze and surprise, he got his straight flush. We all screamed out in shock and excitement. As Erik tried to pass her half his winnings, she was gracious and said, "No, no, you don't have to do that!"

But Erik was firm, "Oh, yes, I do! Clearly I had some help on that one and I'm not going back on my word. Karma would never forgive me."

That had been a fun night.

I entered the room and sat on the bed, wondering how many times Erik and I had stayed in rooms just like this. I saw him sitting in the chair by the window, smiling at me with that tight-lipped grin. *Where are you right now? What are you seeing?* Erik loved to learn and he loved to say, "You don't know what you don't know!" *Are you learning everything you ever wondered about? Are you happy?*

As I sat there, my phone dinged. It was a message from our friend, JR, whom we had just had lunch with. I opened the Facebook Messenger app and clicked on the message from JR:

"I can tell close friends and family by how we forget the time and miles since we have last seen each other, that in a few short moments it's like we just walked next door to say hey. Please share with Erik how much I enjoyed visiting with you both. I feel very blessed to call you both friends. Have a safe trip home."

My heart sunk to my stomach.

I responded, "JR, call me ASAP."

And that's when I formed the narrative of what happened. And just like with the script about my brother Brad, I was able to recite it without actually thinking about what it meant. For the months to come, I couldn't bring myself to say, "when Erik died." The best I could summon was, "when everything happened." Looking back, that description encapsulated the enormity of the events more precisely anyway. His death didn't just affect him, it changed my life and his kids' lives forever. It changed *everything*.

After talking with JR, I called my best friend Dawn and shared the narrative with her. Within a few hours, Marshall and Mandy arrived at the hotel. By this time, I was on full auto pilot mode. Plans and logistics were discussed for the following days but I was diligent in not allowing my mind to go forward in time to contemplate my life without Erik.

Throughout the years, Marshall had become a beloved brother to me. In contrast to Erik, Marshall is tall with a thin build, dirty blond hair, and sharp features. The disparity didn't stop with their looks, they were also on opposite sides politically and socially. However, they had learned to debate respectfully and recognize when it was time to agree to disagree. Also, where Erik was driven to achieve and succeed, Marshall was more relaxed, content with having enough to cover his bills and enjoy life. Despite the overwhelming differences, Erik and Marshall, at their core, were brothers who loved each other and would do anything for the other.

From the very beginning I have always felt very comfortable around Marshall. Perhaps because he has the same cheerful demeanor as my brother. An optimist who rarely gets angry, eager to help others, and full of gratitude.

Marshall met Mandy shortly before we moved to St. Louis, and we were thrilled when they announced their engagement. It was obvious to us immediately when we met her that she was a good fit for Marshall. She's a pretty woman with long dark hair and a round face with kind eyes, with a fun-loving side that mirrored Marshall's, but also a CPA with a stable, successful career.

Once the lights were turned off, Marshall and Mandy occupying the bed next to me, I recognized immediately that the dark silence created too much opportunity for my mind to go to places it was prohibited and so I grabbed my cell phone and the hotel pen and paper and turned my back to Marshall and Mandy to shield them from the flashlight of my phone. To keep my mind occupied, I began making a list of all that I would need to do as a result of everything that happened: Cancel his phone service, call our car insurance, health insurance. I didn't need to worry about life insurance, there was none.

Just the year prior, before we moved from Denver, it had been pressing on me that we needed to get life insurance again. We had had a 10-year term policy that expired a few years prior. When I made the initial call and spoke to a representative, they asked me the typical questions. First I was seeking a quote for Erik and so I was answering questions on his behalf. One of the questions was, does he smoke? My exact words, "He has a cigar occasionally."

The rep replied, "That's no problem. We won't worry about that."

As we progressed with the questions for both Erik and then me, I was then informed the next step would be to have a home nurse visit to take some blood, record our height and weight and so forth. Within the week, a portly, unfriendly older woman arrived at our house and we began the process. She again asked us a set of questions from her clipboard. She asked

Erik if he used tobacco. We gave the exact same answer, "He has a cigar occasionally."

We were shocked when we found out the following week that he had been denied for lying on his application. We were informed that the first rep we spoke to put down "no" for smoking, and the nurse had recorded "Yes." I was livid. Erik, more familiar with the way insurance companies work, explained that correcting the contradicting answers would be a burdensome task and a time-consuming process. Our hands full already with packing and getting ready for our move to St. Louis, it got put on the back burner. I assumed there was no urgency since we were only 42 years old at that time. What were the odds that something would happen? We had plenty of time to take care of it later. Sadly, "later" didn't happen.

All night long I made list after list. When I finished one, I would start another, often writing down the same things. I could hear Marshall breathing heavily in his sleep in the bed next to me and I told myself it was Erik. It was easy because it sounded just like him.

By 3 a.m. I could barely keep my eyes open. Sensing it was safe to turn off the light, I set the list aside and allowed myself to fall into a dreamless, deep sleep.

The Next Day

I awoke roughly three hours later and rolled over to my other side. It took a few seconds to register that something wasn't right. *Where am I? Wait. Erik.* It started coming back. The Tahoe bouncing through the desert, Erik in the view of the truck window. *Nope, I'm not going there.* I threw the covers off and headed to the shower, allowing Marshall and Mandy to sleep.

After I had checked in the day prior, I visited the hotel gift shop because I needed contact solution and a case to put my contacts in. From all the crying and standing in a windy desert, my eyes were extremely dry and uncomfortable. I looked for something I could change into as well, maybe sweatpants or different shorts, but the hotel was severely lacking in appropriate attire for women who were stranded after their husband's death. I was in no mood to wear anything bedazzled.

And so here I was in the exact same clothes, my white trouser shorts from Banana Republic and orange cotton camisole from Ann Taylor. After Mandy and Marshall roused and got ready, we made our way to the airport to pick up my sister. We found the baggage claim area and waited near the one where her suitcase would be coming down. *Kathy, hold it together.* Just knowing my sister would be with me in just a few minutes made my eyes begin to water. She was one of the few people I felt comfortable crying in front of. But I knew if I started again, it would be a repeat of the back of the police car. I didn't want that attention. I didn't want that pain. *Not now. I just can't.*

As soon as I saw my sister and we locked eyes I knew I was in trouble. As she walked up to me, the look of pain and sympathy and love was almost too much to bear. I could see her eyes starting to well up. *I can't do this.* Before she even could hug me, I said sternly, "Nope, we're not going there."

I gave her a quick hug and we waited for her suitcase. I felt bad that I was behaving so coldly but it was pure survival and self-preservation. I wasn't ready and I couldn't bear to break down like I had in the police car. That had been excruciating.

It was decided the night before that we would meet Erik's aunt and cousins at his cousin Krissy's house. I would need to finalize things with Erik's remains and collect my items from the Tahoe. Also, since California had been Erik's home his whole life, it only made sense that we would have his memorial service there.

Krissy has a comfortable home in Yucaipa, a typical 1980s southern California stucco home, three bedroom/two bath, but beautifully decorated since Krissy had been an interior decorator. They brought in chairs from the dining room so we all had a place to sit in the cozy living room and we talked about what we wanted to do. I knew from conversations with Erik that he would expect to be cremated, and so I shared that with the family.

As I sat there and listened to the family chat about venues and caterers, I could feel Erik sitting next to me, arms crossed with his fingers stuck in his armpits, just his thumb sticking out, and leaning over and whispering to me, "Just throw me in the oven and have a nice thought."

I had to stifle a laugh. It had been kind of a personal joke between us. We were sitting on the front patio when Erik mentioned he had spoken to his old friend Scottie from Palm Springs. "Scottie's dad passed away this week."

"Oh, shoot, that stinks." I had commented.

"Are they planning a funeral?" I asked.

"Nah, Scottie just said, we'll just throw him in the oven and have a nice thought."

I had burst out laughing. It absolutely sounded like something Scottie would say, but I had to ask, "Did he really say that?"

Erik came clean, "No, he didn't say that."

But from then on, when we talked about our own passing, we would joke, "Just throw me in the oven and have a nice thought."

For obvious reasons, now didn't seem like an appropriate time to share that.

The whole week that followed was about distractions. Planning Erik's memorial service was a great distraction. Although, with Erik's absence, it felt more like a surprise party.

We checked out venues and picked a caterer and menu. Erik's cousin Jason was a pastor at a local church and so they allowed us to hold the service there. My sister and I were invited to Aunt Nancy's for the week while we planned, and it couldn't have been a better place for me at that time. The familiarity of her home from sharing numerous past holidays and birthday celebrations provided me with the sense that Erik was just in the next room, never far away.

While the days' activities varied during the following week, depending on which family member was arriving from out of state, the mornings and evenings remained fairly consistent. My day typically started between 5 and 6 a.m., as soon as my eyes opened, which was usually after about four hours of sleep. I hesitated only long enough in bed for my mind to grasp that it was another day without Erik, spurring me to get up and make my way to the kitchen. Aunt Nancy would have the coffee all ready to go and so I just had to turn the coffee pot on and wait for the aroma of the beans to fill my nose. As soon as there was enough in the pot, I would carefully fill my cup and return the pot to continue its function. I would then wrap my hands around the warm mug and walk out the back sliding glass door to the covered patio. This became my sanctuary.

As I absorbed the morning sun and quietness, the view of Aunt Nancy's backyard was nothing but tranquility. I watched squirrels run and jump from the large mature trees that surrounded her yard, providing privacy that was much appreciated. Rabbits hopped in and out of the flowering bushes along the sides of the property, seemingly unaware of my presence, or, at the very least, not threatened by it. Sitting at the patio table, with my knees up to my chest and hugging my coffee mug, listening to the birds, I felt safe to just *be*. Physical exhaustion made the task of not thinking an easy one.

It wouldn't take long and Aunt Nancy would be the second to rise. After pouring her own cup of heavenly caffeine, she would join me outside. Aunt Nancy is a no-nonsense kind of lady in her 70s, originally from New Jersey and so she has no problem telling you how it is. She's not going to sugar-coat anything and she's not throwing anyone a big ol' pity party. She was exactly what I needed.

As fate would have it, she had lost her husband on the exact same date as Erik exactly 15 years prior. He had died after a short battle with cancer, also way too young. She understood grief and survival and she didn't tiptoe around me. I feel like whatever I would have done, even if I had sat there and bawled all morning, she would have been okay with it and she would have sat with me and let me have whatever moment I needed to have.

Aunt Nancy also knew how to read me in the mornings. Sometimes we would just sit together in the quietness. Sometimes she would impart welcome bits of wisdom, things she had learned from her life experiences. Sometimes we just chatted about what was planned for the upcoming day. I didn't need words from her to know how she was feeling. And she didn't need words from me for her to know how I was feeling. There was just a mutual love and understanding of each other and what each of us had suffered. I hadn't spent much one-on-one time with Aunt Nancy before this. Our encounters were usually family celebrations or holidays, but I always enjoyed her matter-of-fact demeanor. I'm so grateful that I was given the opportunity to get to know her in this way.

The other half of my routine was night time. After sharing dinner with varying family members, depending on who had arrived in town and who was available, and after the kitchen was cleaned, dishes put away, everyone had gone home, and the kitchen lights dimmed, my sister and I would be the last ones up at night.

My Siblings

Sherry is 8 years my senior, and so while my brother, Terry, and I were playing rubber band wars, she was busy with high school activities of band, chorus, friends, and boys. She was a 5-foot-2, blond-haired, blue-eyed beauty and I thought she was the coolest person ever. I never passed up an opportunity to be around her, even if it meant driving to McDonald's with her to pick up dinner. I loved sitting with her in the front seat of her brightly painted blue 1968 Ford Galaxy 500, listening to her sing along to Styx or Supertramp. She made me feel like a girlfriend, not an annoying little sister.

One evening before dinner, when I was 8 years old, my sister was in her room and she was allowing me to hang out with her, a rare occurrence just because she was so rarely home.

"Kathy, you have to hear this new song!" She declared.

Right away I was filled with excitement that my big sister wanted to share something with me. She then proceeded to play Barracuda by Heart. As we listened and she sang along to it, I had no idea what the song was about, but I never wanted to forget that moment or that song.

After Sherry graduated from high school, she attended the local University of North Dakota and moved into the dorms and so I saw her even less, but she did her best to keep a relationship with me by inviting me to stay for a night in the dorm with her. We would make popcorn and watch movies and she would introduce me to her friends. What I was too young to realize at that time was that she was planting the seeds to a relationship that would grow and blossom into something that gets more and more beautiful every year. A bond that has survived time, distance, and squabbles. We haven't always shared the same views, but we've always valued family, and so we celebrate our similarities and we agree to disagree on our differences.

Not long after graduating college, Sherry married her husband, Tom, and in quick succession they had all four of their children. It had been important for Sherry to stay at home with her kids and so Tom worked hard to make that possible. He had started as a cable installer before they were married, but then had climbed the ranks through the years. This required a couple of moves, one of them to South Dakota, but it didn't take them long to realize they were homesick and they found their way back to Minnesota.

Through all of her moves and all of mine, Sherry and I always stayed close. Regardless of our financial situations, we both found ways to see each other at least once or twice a year.

At my sister's core, she is a giver. Nothing brings her more joy than being helpful and providing assistance wherever needed, whether that's delivering a meal to someone or offering a shoulder to cry on. Once she recognizes a need, she will go out of her way to provide it.

That's why it didn't surprise me at all when Sherry said she would be on the next plane. If she is determined to make something happen, it happens. She was heartbroken that she couldn't be there any sooner than the following morning.

My brother, on the other hand, despite urging from his wife, determined it wasn't financially possible for him to come to California. It wasn't surprising, but it was disappointing not to have him there.

Growing up, Terry and I enjoyed a close relationship. Being two and a half years older than me, I looked up to my big brother and he was always very loving towards me. On Saturday mornings we would lie on the couch together and watch cartoons. In the wintertime, we made caves out of the snowbanks and had snowball fights. I always felt like I could count on my brother to be there for me.

When I was 14 years old, one night while mom and dad were out bowling, some friends and I thought it would be fun to sneak some of my parents' alcohol. My brother, who had been at work, came home to a group of drunk kids. He proceeded to do what not many big brothers would do, he piled my friends into his old, ginormous Impala, put their bikes in his trunk, and drove them all home. Then he came home, helped me take my contacts out, put me to bed, and cleaned up the mess. My parents were none the wiser.

And that wouldn't be the only time he rescued me.

When I was 15 years old, my dad allowed me to take some friends in his El Camino to a boy's house that lived out in the country. I didn't have my license yet, but my dad had been driving with me since I was 12 and felt comfortable with my driving skills, I guess, or perhaps he felt guilty about leaving my mother and me. Either way, I couldn't wait to take the car out with my friends. The El Camino only allowed for three people max and so I had a friend sitting next to me in the middle and another friend on the opposite side of her, near the window.

As we drove down the dirt road to the house, we came to a somewhat sharp curve in the road. The friend that was sitting next to me had her left leg near mine. As we approached the curve, she feared we were going too fast and panicked, slamming her foot down to brace herself and grabbing the wheel. The El Camino took a sharp turn right into the adjacent corn field, and as we all screamed, corn was flying everywhere. My friends yelled at me, "Stop! Kathy, stop!"

I was pressing the brake as hard as I could but nothing was happening. Then I looked down and realized that my friend's foot was slammed against the gas pedal.

"Lorri! Move your foot!" I hollered.

Finally, we came to a stop about a quarter of a mile into the middle of the corn field. After collecting ourselves and bringing our breathing back to normal, we decided to get out and survey the damage. However, the corn was so tight around us, we could barely open the car doors against the large stalks. After we squeezed out of the car, we turned around and saw the path of destruction we had just created. For some reason, maybe just from relief that we weren't hurt, we broke into hysterics, laughing until our sides hurt and tears ran down our faces. The perfectly flattened corn the exact width of the car, creating a wall of corn on each side, is permanently etched in my memory.

To my relief, we were able to get the car out of the cornfield, and we all decided it would be best just to go back home. We had had enough excitement for one day. However, I noticed on the way home that the steering wheel was difficult to turn. It felt like we were dragging corn stalks behind the car. The closer we got to home, the more fearful I was of what my dad was going to say when he found out. Surely, he would never let me take the car again.

Thankfully, my brother was home when I brought the car back. Before telling Dad about the car, I asked my brother for some advice.

"Tell Dad that you started to lose control of the car on the dirt road, and that instead of hitting a culvert, you hit the corn field."

I had no idea what a culvert was, but I trusted my big brother. I rehearsed exactly what Terry said, and when I told it to my dad, he patted me on the shoulder and said, "That's good, sweetie. You did the right thing."

After that and throughout high school, Terry was my friend as much as he was my brother. His friends and my friends often congregated in my dad's basement, shooting pool and drinking more than we should.

Sadly, after I moved away, Terry and I weren't very good at staying in touch. Our relationship consisted of two phone calls a year: one on his birthday in February and one on mine in September. However, whenever I went home, the love and friendship always remained. We always made a point to spend time together to catch up on our lives.

I have come to accept that my brother is a simple guy. He is probably the happiest, go-with-the-flow man you will ever meet. He's worked at the same mattress factory for most of his adult life now, and even though the pay isn't much, he's comfortable there, and he's a good worker so his bosses value him. And somehow, with the help of his wife, Terry has always managed to provide for his family, which consists of four kids from Rhonda's previous marriage, and one daughter that Terry and Rhonda share. They live in the modular home that my father purchased, and they now run the cemetery. Terry, at 50 years old, had never owned a cell phone. He just didn't see the need.

And in my brother's simpleness there is a heart of gold. He is a guy that loves with his whole heart. He has a deep faith in God and does his very best to live a life that matches his beliefs.

However, when Terry declared that he wasn't coming to Erik's memorial service, it made me question our relationship, his love for me. I began to resent him, even though deep down I knew he loved me.

Later, during my months of grieving and spending time with God, He healed that hurt by showing me that my brother's response to my grief wasn't about me. Whatever reasons he had for not coming, that was about him. It had nothing to do with how much he loved me. I could not allow my expectations of him to stain our relationship. I learned that I needed to love him for who he was and accept him for who he was not.

The Kindness of Others

At Aunt Nancy's, in the evenings, Sherry and I would sit in the 1990s kitchen with the lights dimmed at the wooden kitchen table. We would talk about me, we would talk about her, we would talk about our parents. She was a familiar and comfortable presence and I don't know what I would have done without her. We would stay up until midnight or 1 a.m., somehow finding new things to share with each other that the other hadn't known. When she finally tired out, she would say her good-nights and head off to bed.

I was usually tired by that time but not tired enough. I had to time my bed time correctly or else I might succumb to another sob fest that I still wasn't ready for. I needed to be so tired that I would fall asleep instantly, no time for thinking. And so while everyone else was dreaming dreams and rolling over in their warm, comfy beds, I decided that in order to further distract myself, I would send out texts to friends and family, updating them on the plans for Erik's memorial service, with the expectation and hope that people had their phones turned to silent so that I wouldn't wake anyone. And no group texts. It took more time to type out each text individually and that was fine with me. I was just passing the time anyway.

On the first night that I began sending texts out, I cringed when my phone dinged with a response. *Oh, shoot, I woke someone up.* It was Robin, of course.

"Do you want to talk?" She texted me.

I closed my eyes and heaved a heavy sigh. Sometimes I was just overwhelmed by the kindness and selflessness of some of the people in my life. It was humbling to say the least.

"I would love to." I texted back.

"Give me a minute to get downstairs so I don't wake up John," her husband.

For the next hour or so we would chat about the update, what I had done that day, about life, about death. Sometimes she just listened to me ramble about things that exhausted people ramble about....nothing. And when I finally had difficulty keeping my eyes open, I would thank her and she would tell me to go to bed. For that whole week, Robin went to bed and kept her cell phone next to her, not turned on silent, just in case I texted. And every night I texted and every night she texted right back, "Do you want to talk?"

The love and support that I received during that week was, and still is, overwhelming. At one point Tosha noticed I wasn't eating and started to randomly feed me protein bars. I even found them in my purse, where she had placed them in case I got hungry when we were out.

My sister's husband, Tom, and their kids Riley, Taylor, and Haley flew in from Minnesota. Riley was at training for the reserves, usually unreachable during those weeks, but they found a way to get a message to him and he was granted leave. To afford the flights, they took multiple layovers and spent most of a day bouncing on and off airplanes. They did that just for me.

Marshall and Mandy flew in Tyler, who was living in Arizona at that time.

Erik's cousins, Krissy and Jason and Jason's wife Kris, were amazing. They were integral in putting the service together. They were the perfect amount of taking over and still involving me. They got the photos together, planned the music, they even made me a photo book of Erik's life. We had always had a good relationship, even a friendship, and so I trusted their judgement on all of the arrangements, knowing that we shared the same tastes.

The day before the memorial service, it had occurred to me that I hadn't cried all that week. There were even times when I felt like I should have cried, like when we were picking up my belongings from the Tahoe or when I had to pick up the items that Erik had on him when he passed; his watch, his wallet, his wedding ring, which were handed to me in a plastic Ziploc bag. I recognized that I should be crying, and yet not a tear. *What the heck is wrong with me? Come on, Kathy, people are watching and expecting you to cry!* But I just accepted the baggie, studied the contents for a minute, and put it in my purse. *Okay, I look like the worst wife in the world right now.* But there was nothing I could do. I literally could not force myself to cry. It was like I had grief constipation. I had pushed the grief away for so long, it was no longer accessible.

Then I started to worry, what if I didn't cry at Erik's memorial service? Oh, my gosh, that would be terrible! The thought of that really started to bother me. The evening before the memorial service, after dinner with Erik's family, I asked Jason if we could go for a walk. Jason was a former surfer dude, rock'n roller, become Christian. He was in his late 30s and so he easily related to the younger congregants at his church, but he was also old enough that older generations also felt comfortable being counseled by him.

It was a beautiful evening in Redlands, where Aunt Nancy's house is. She lives in an older section of town but it's kept beautiful by the manicured landscaping and nicely maintained homes. As Jason and I walked, I shared what I had observed the past week about my inability to cry. I said, "Jason, what if I don't cry at Erik's service?"

Jason's response was swift and gentle, a beacon of wisdom in my moment of uncertainty. "Kathy, if you feel peace right now, take it. You may not always have it."

Just like that, the weight was lifted off my shoulders. Of course. I would grieve in my way and my time. It didn't matter what other people thought. From that moment on, I resolved to honor my emotions authentically, regardless of others' expectations.

The day of Erik's service I stood in front of the bathroom mirror wearing the same black dress I had worn just 2 weeks prior when Erik and I had celebrated our 15th wedding anniversary. Again. Technically we had two anniversaries. We had officially gotten married in January that year, but our church wedding was May 29 and so we mostly celebrated that one.

Remembering Our Marriage

This current trip to California was kicked off with a stop in Las Vegas first. We couldn't think of a better place to celebrate our 15th wedding anniversary than the city we were first married in. I slipped into my favorite little black dress which always got a look of approval from Erik, and we headed to a new trendy steakhouse for dinner where we were seated at a small table top for two. It was crowded and buzzing with chatter from nearby tables, creating a fun and light atmosphere. As we sat down at the table, we were both looking forward to a scrumptious meal, relaxing evening, a fantastic week, and the rest of our amazing lives together. As we waited for our food, Erik sipped on a Coke while I enjoyed a nice glass of pinot noir.

For some reason, whenever I drink wine, my arms think they need to step in and assist me while I talk, adding drama and comedy to my stories, I guess. And as usually happens, I accidentally tipped over my glass of water. Since it was such a small table, it immediately formed a river and a waterfall off the table. Erik reacted quickly and used his napkin to stop the flow and simultaneously flagged a bus boy for some help as he explained, "I tipped over my water. Would you mind helping?"

And I leaned back in my chair and smiled. That was Erik and that was why I loved him. He took the blame for me without even a thought. How many husbands would have said, "My clumsy wife, who likes to talk with her hands after a few sips of wine, just spilled her water."

And this is what made our marriage work. There was no keeping score. There was no, "I took the garbage out last night. It's your turn." If the trash needed to be taken out, one of us just did it. There was a time I started getting annoyed that Erik was constantly leaving his cereal boxes on the countertop after he would finish pouring a bowl. It could be an empty box or new box, didn't matter. For whatever reason, the box remained on the counter. Every time I walked into the kitchen and saw the Honey Comb box, I would think, *Seriously? It would take 2 seconds to put it away.*

And then one day I happened to look out the window that looked onto our driveway. It was winter and cold out, and I saw Erik outside at the side of my car, leaning over the windshield. He had noticed that my windshield wipers were starting to wear and so he purchased new ones and he was replacing them for me. I hadn't asked him to do that. Gratitude mixed with a touch of shame settled in my chest. It made me reconsider my reaction to the cereal boxes. After that, every time I walked into the kitchen and saw a box of Honey Comb, I remembered the windshield wipers, and I felt happy that I could put the box away for him.

And now here I was standing in front of a mirror wearing that same black dress and Erik was gone. *How can your life change so quickly?* I asked myself again for the millionth time. Yet knowing I would never have an answer.

Saying Goodbye

After everyone was ready to go to the church, we all piled into cars. I rode with Krissy and Aunt Nancy in her 2012 Honda Pilot. Sitting in the back behind the passenger seat, I looked out the window and stared at nothing. A heaviness began to settle in my chest in anticipation of what may or may not happen.

And then God told me, *It's not for you to wonder why, but to be thankful for what you had.*

It was like when 15 *years* popped into my head when I found Taffy. Of course, now I knew that it meant I would have Erik for 15 *years* instead of Taffy.

And I knew for a fact that I hadn't just conjured up this new message. And those may not have been the exact words, but that was the intent. Again, I don't necessarily hear a voice or words, but I know when I'm told something I didn't previously know or think about. When somebody tells you something, you may not remember the exact words they said to you, but you remember the meaning of their message.

I hadn't realized it at the time, but God had been speaking to me for years. I'm not sure when it started, but at some point after Erik and I married, whenever I had an option of doing something with Erik or doing something else, I would always think, pick your husband, you never know how much time you have together. And it wasn't a morbid, oh, my gosh, he's going to die. It was very matter-of-fact. It was similar to thinking that I should lock my car when I go into the mall because someone could try to steal it. I really thought nothing about it, but I've never had that feeling or those thoughts about anyone else since then.

When we pulled up to the church, we pulled up to the front so that we could empty the car of all the photos and things we needed for the service. I noticed that a few people were starting to show up. The heaviness in my chest grew.

Needing to feel helpful, I went to the back of the SUV to help Krissy gather items necessary for the service. As she removed different bags from the vehicle, a large head shot of Erik appeared that I wasn't expecting. When I saw his face, his eyes looking right into mine, I had to turn away. *Oh, my gosh. This is real. Erik isn't here.* I put my hand over my mouth. I sucked in air in an attempt to keep my tears at bay. *No, not now. I'm not ready.* I started to walk towards the church, away from the photo, away from Erik. Our good friend Jeff, who had started out as our accountant, came to me and allowed me to hide my face in his shoulder. I was relieved I could contain myself to soft crying, and part of me was relieved that I could release some of what had been building up.

Within a few minutes I was able to collect myself and I was shown to the front of the auditorium, where I would be sitting with Tosha on one side of me and Tyler on the other. We were there early so that we could privately view the slide show that Erik's cousins had put together, set to the song by Jon Foreman, "Behind Your Eyes." When Krissy had shared with me that they were working on that, I had asked for a private viewing first. I knew it was going to be difficult to watch, and I knew I needed to have an honest reaction to it, not worrying about what people expected or feeling like I was being watched. I invited Tosha and Tyler to share that with me. The time had come for me to step out of the world of make-believe. I couldn't pretend that Erik was still here anymore. I needed to face the reality of my life now.

The music started and photos started flashing up: Erik as a baby, playing in a small plastic swimming pool. Erik as a

133

young boy with the 1970s haircut and bell bottoms. Erik as a teenager at an air show in San Diego with his little brother, tan and shirtless and looking like a teen heartthrob. Erik with his baby girl Tosha, throwing her up in the air as a toddler. Erik with Tyler as a 5-year-old in front of a Christmas tree. Even at that young age, the resemblance was remarkable.

I felt it coming but this time I allowed it. I knew I needed it. I let the sobs out that had been hiding all week. I covered my face with my hands and leaned over my lap. I felt Tosha's and Tyler's arms on my back, comforting me. Again I endured the physical pain in my chest that competed to match the emotional pain I was feeling. I felt safe with Tosha and Tyler with me. We had been in each other's lives for 15 years and I loved them with my whole heart. They had accepted me from day one and welcomed me into the family with such love. I had watched them grow from silly, fun little kids to mature and loving adults. My heart broke for them just as much as it did for me. Tosha had just found out she was pregnant the day before. Erik would have been a grandfather, which he would have absolutely loved. Did I mention that life isn't fair?

After our private viewing, as the ceremony started, Jason's wife, Kris, began to play the piano and sing. She has one of the most amazing voices I have ever heard, and I have always been so in awe of her talent. Today I wasn't thinking about that, I was letting the melody and her voice soothe me and calm my nerves. It was like slowly submerging into warm water, reaching every part of me. I felt the tears sliding down my cheeks, but it was okay, they were sad tears but not devastated tears. Erik deserved every single one of them.

After they played the slide show, family and friends got up to speak, share stories of Erik. I would listen and smile, and then I would look over at the large photo of Erik that was on an easel in front of me. His eyes were so blue and they looked right at you. *Oh, Erik. Why did you leave me? How am I going to do this on my own? Are you here right now? Can you see all the people here and how much you were loved?*

I couldn't stop looking at him. How was it even possible that this was happening?

After the ceremony was over, after the reception that followed, after all the condolences were handed out and accepted, after everyone went home, that was when the real work of grieving started.

Next Steps

Throughout the week there had been one question that everyone asked me: Are you going to stay in St. Louis. It was a question that floated around my brain all week. It was a question loaded with considerations. Although I had no ties to the city beyond my job and my affection for it, the thought of leaving raised a flurry of thoughts. My roots lay in Minnesota, where most of my family resided, yet the bitter winters there held little appeal. New York beckoned with its allure and friendships, but its exorbitant cost of living and notorious traffic dampened the appeal. California, with its familial connections, tugged at my heartstrings, but the thought of returning to its high costs and congested roads made me hesitate. That leaves the last city I lived in, Denver. I had Erik's brother and family there, plus my dear friend Chandra and her family, but I didn't enjoy my work there as much.

Then I remembered what Erik's Aunt Nancy told me one morning as we shared our coffee together: Don't make any major decisions for one year. The minute she said that, I felt a huge weight lifted. It felt right. I could do that. I could stay for a year.

Before returning to St. Louis after Erik's memorial, I needed to fly to Denver. Erik and I had driven to Marshall's from St. Louis so that he could care for Kira while we were gone. I would need to gather Kira and drive back to St. Louis. From the moment I realized that this would require a full day's drive by myself, I knew I couldn't do it alone, and I knew there was only one person who I could do this drive with, my best friend, Dawn.

Throughout the years I have known Dawn, she has gone from my boyfriend's sister to a dear friend and eventually to an honorary sister. Despite the miles between us, our bond remained unbreakable. Our sporadic conversations would effortlessly bridge the gaps in time, knitting our lives together with laughter, tears, and unwavering support.

When I met Dawn, I was 21 and she was 27. I was still trying to figure out what I wanted to do with my life and she was at the beginning of her career. I looked up to her, and I was in awe of her independence. She had had boyfriends at different times, but she admitted to me once that she didn't think she would ever marry. *Never marry??* That was such a foreign concept to me. I had never met anybody that didn't want to get married. Yet she was so matter-of-fact about it. She hadn't ruled it out, it just wasn't a concern. Even as independent as I thought I was, I knew I wanted to be married someday.

Dawn also had faith that I hadn't witnessed before. To me, she exuded God's love and peace, and each time I was with her, I felt that the light that surrounded her would also encircle me. It felt warm and safe.

I was so relieved when Tim and I broke up and we remained friends. She has seen me through some crazy twists and turns throughout my life. The summer that I met Erik and decided to move to California, it had been such a whirlwind that I hadn't spoken to any of my friends. When I returned to New York after being in Minnesota, Dawn and Glenda (Dawn's sister) invited me over because we had all agreed to head a youth group at our local parish and we needed to start the planning process. I decided to wait until I was with them before I shared the news.

Once I arrived and the usual hugs and greetings were exchanged, we gathered around the small kitchen table to dive into our planning. Before we went any further, I said, "I won't be able to do the youth group with you."

They looked at me with casual interest. I took a deep breath.

"I met a guy on the internet and I'm moving to California and getting married."

Wide eyes and crickets.

Dawn's perfect response, "I'll get the wine."

Needless to say, that became the topic of the night. In fact, the topic of many nights. As I made plans and started packing and saying my goodbyes, nearly everyone tried to talk sense into me. I didn't mind because they were right. It was crazy! But the day that Dawn and I sat on the field near my apartment, watching Taffy romp around, is forever etched in my memory. As we chatted about my upcoming move, there were no words of caution, no attempts to talk me out of it. She didn't just accept that this was what I was going to do, she understood and she supported me. I was filled with gratitude that someone else could see God in all of this.

In the years that have passed, Dawn has become a confidant and wise and trusted counselor. Whenever I've come to her with different problems or issues, she doesn't tell me what I should do, she asks me questions, and she listens. She includes God in our conversation, reminding me to seek His guidance. Dawn helps me to find the most loving way to approach any situation. That's why I knew she had to be one to drive with me back to St. Louis. And when I asked her, there wasn't a pause or a thought, of course she would do that.

The day after Erik's memorial service, I flew back to Colorado with Marshall and Mandy. As we entered Marshall's house, I could see that Kira was outside on the back deck and was anxious to say hello. Seeing her so excited was heartwarming and heartbreaking at the same time. As I stepped out onto the patio to greet her, she couldn't contain her joy. Her large body twisted and bounced as she pressed her head into my legs and spoke cries of excitement. I bent over her and hugged whatever parts I could grab until she finally calmed down and I could give her a proper squeeze.

When we opened the patio door and entered the house, Kira ran to Erik's suitcase that we had brought into the house, and then she darted up the stairs and ran into each bedroom, again searching for a friend she would never find. It broke my heart all over again.

Dawn arrived the next day and we rose early the following morning to get on the road so that the majority of the drive would be done in daylight. As we entered the highway that would take us across Colorado and straight through Missouri, I couldn't help but feel like I was on the road to the rest of my life. Dawn offered to take the first shift of driving and so with Kira comfortable in the back, I decided to get comfortable for the long drive. I slipped off my sandals and tucked my legs under me Indian style. As I did so, I paused. My mind went back to the rental car in the desert. They were the same sandals that I struggled to put on after Erik....well, after everything happened. For a second, I recalled the panic and how I had regretted taking them off that day. I considered putting them back on in case something happened again. *No, you're not going to think like that.*

So much of that drive is a blur for me now. What I remember is feeling peace and calmness, gratitude for a friend that I could share my thoughts with, a friend who always had loving and gentle responses, and who could also be silent and thoughtful. I was relieved to be going home, but at the same time I felt apprehensive about how I would feel walking into the last house that Erik and I shared together, even though we had only lived there a month. Would it trigger another sobbing spree? I truly hoped not.

Surprisingly, as we got closer to the house, I didn't feel dread or anxiety. Dawn was the perfect distraction. Had I been doing this alone, I can almost guarantee that that wouldn't be the case. It wasn't until the house came into view that I felt my stomach turn a bit. Our street consisted of a big square pattern, and our house was situated at the end of one of the streets. As we drove up the street, our house dead ahead, in complete view, and our large wicker chairs were visible on the front porch, peeking out from behind the hedge that spanned the length of the patio, creating a barrier to the front yard. I could see Erik sitting in one of the chairs, just as I had seen him many of the nights since we moved there. After dinner, I would often walk Kira around the neighborhood, and as we would complete the circle, we would walk down the street that Dawn and I were driving on, and Erik would be waiting for us on the patio.

I blinked and he disappeared.

Walking into the home was much easier than I anticipated. We occupied ourselves with the task of unloading the Tahoe and preparing for bed and I was able to avoid any painful memories, at least for the time being.

The house we moved into had a master suite plus two other bedrooms and another full bath. The two extra bedrooms had beds but I hadn't had a chance to make them up. Mostly because there hadn't been a need. And I didn't see the need to do it that night either. Our master bedroom had a newly purchased Tempur-Pedic queen sized bed and so Dawn and I had no problems sharing a bed. I was still in the practice of waiting until complete exhaustion before attempting to lay down, and so after Dawn went to sleep, I turned on the TV. The long drive must have worn me out more than I thought because it didn't take long for me to find it difficult to keep my eyes open. That was my cue that I was ready. Except when I lay down next to Dawn, who was soundly sleeping, sleep did not happen for me. Instead, memories started tumbling into my head, causing my chest to tighten. *Nope. Not sleeping here.*

I decided to make up the bed in the far bedroom near the front of the house. It was the next largest room and also where we had placed my dressers and hung up my clothes. What began as my closet room became my official bedroom from that night forward. I never slept in the master bedroom again..

Dawn had a week before she had to return to Connecticut, and so it was easy to see where we needed to focus our time. I needed to make this home feel less like Erik and Kathy and more just Kathy. Each day consisted of sharing morning coffee on the patio, and then tackling a different room to convert into a space that would feel like home to me. We purchased window treatments and a few needed pieces of furniture, plant stands, wall hangings, and decorative pillows. She helped me rearrange the furniture to make the room more inviting and appealing. Dawn has a great eye for decorating and so I valued her help and suggestions.

The days flew by and when evening came, we were proud of our progress, and I was amazed to see the transformation. Without spending a ton of money, we had changed the whole feel of the house. It went from empty and impersonal to warm and cozy. After dinner we would sit on the front porch, wine in hand, and congratulate ourselves on a productive day. We would also talk about things that maybe came up that day regarding Erik's passing.

On one of the days, we journeyed into his closet to inspect the safe I knew we had stored there. I also was keenly aware that I had no idea what the combination was. Something caused Dawn to inspect the safe, and when she pulled on the door, to our shock and dismay, the door opened. It appeared that Erik had shut the door but hadn't engaged the lock. I couldn't believe it. That was not like Erik at all to be so careless, especially when we would be gone for so long. Of course, Dawn and I just looked at each other and smiled. God at work, of course!

Other than opening the safe, I wasn't ready to tackle Erik's closet or even the master bedroom. I didn't even feel it was an option. I had already erased most of him throughout the house, I didn't want to get rid of him completely. At least not yet.

When the time came for Dawn to leave, I think we both felt comfortable in saying that it was time. She had her life to get back to, and I needed to begin mine. I had no idea what that looked like yet, but that was okay. I had no illusions that it was going to be easy, yet I knew the grieving process was going to be necessary and important. When my mother passed away, at the reception I heard so many people say that she had died of a broken heart because after my father left is when my mother's health started to deteriorate. I would not allow history to repeat itself.

The Chore of Grieving

The weeks and months that followed Erik's accident were the most difficult of my life. Questions ran through my head in a constant loop: *What was to become of my life? Could I really stay in St. Louis with no friends or family nearby?* I couldn't work because I couldn't focus. I couldn't watch TV because I didn't care. I couldn't listen to music because music just made me cry. What I could do is read. I read every book I could get my hands on about grief and grieving. Reading and praying took up the majority of my days. When I couldn't do any of those, I would just sit, as I did at Aunt Nancy's, and just be.

One book in particular proved exceptionally valuable: "A Grace Disguised: How the Soul Grows Through Loss" by Jerry Sittser. His poignant account of losing his wife, mother, and daughter in a tragic accident resonated deeply. Despite unimaginable suffering, he found peace and purpose, emphasizing the importance of not allowing loss to define one's identity. His words echoed within me: "The experience of loss itself does not have to be the defining moment of our lives. Instead, the defining moment can be *our response* to the loss. It is not what happens *to us* that matters as much as what happens *in us.*"

Another insight struck a chord: the acknowledgment that we may not miss every aspect of the person we lost. While initially feeling irreverent or even disrespectful, it rang true. I couldn't deny that amidst my grief, I didn't miss Erik's temper and walking on eggshells when I knew he was in a bad mood. Conversely, I realized that there were traits of mine he wouldn't miss either.

A topic that intrigued me now was near-death experiences, yearning to understand where Erik was and what he was experiencing. I've heard it said many times that it is but a thin veil that separates us from the hereafter. I realized how true that was one morning a few months after Erik had passed:

I had enjoyed a deep, dreamless sleep that night, but just as the sun began to shine through my window, I was dreaming that a white kitten was near my face and sniffing my mouth. The feeling woke me. As my thoughts began to arouse me out of sleep, I sensed a familiar smell. Within just a few seconds I knew exactly what I was smelling. It was Erik. I knew I wasn't imagining it because it's not a scent you keep in your recall, like cinnamon or coffee. I knew the smell because I woke up next to it for 15 years.

My eyes remained closed, fearful he would disappear if he knew I was awake. I lay there frozen for several minutes. *Oh, Erik I know this is you. Thank you for visiting me.* And then he was gone. This experience didn't scare me at all. I felt peace from it because I felt Erik was at peace. I think he wanted me to know he was okay.

During the grief process, I learned the necessity of allowing myself a daily cry. I also learned that if I didn't instigate it myself, it would ambush me like Kato on the Pink Panther.

The first time I learned this was on a trip to the grocery store. I thought I had been doing so well, I had gone almost a whole day without crying. I picked up a few items in the produce area and as I was making my way through the store, I found myself cutting through the cereal aisle. And there it was, my eyes went right to it. I wasn't even looking for it. The box of Honey Comb reached out and grabbed me by the shirt collar with two fists and shook me, screaming LOOK AT ME! LOOK AT ME! The aisle started to close in on me and all I could think was *I miss putting his cereal away.*

I had no choice in the matter, tears were coming and they were coming NOW. I left my basket in the cereal aisle and rushed to my car so I could suffer the cry fest in privacy. From that day on, I made it a point every day to sit down with the book that Erik's cousins had made me, play some music, and get my crying out of the way so that I could go about my day. Within a few weeks, I noticed I could skip a day, and then a couple days, and eventually I was able to look at the book without tears and only gratitude for what I had had.

On one of my late summer evening walks with Kira, as we strolled slowly, taking in the beauty of the neighborhood, the towering trees, the thoughtfully planted flowers and freshly mowed lawns, I let my mind wander a bit. Peace and contentment joined me as we walked, but loneliness had also snuck into the group and was trying to get my attention. Thoughts began to meander around my brain, wondering if my future held another marriage in it. I felt disassociated from the thought, as though I was reading the book of my life and wondering what the next chapter was going to be about. As the thought began to take hold, though, I remembered the list I made all those years ago before I met Erik. The thought exhausted me now. *God, if you want me to marry again, he's just got to be everything Erik was and everything Erik wasn't.* That was it. I felt relieved that I didn't have to occupy myself with those thoughts anymore. It was God's now.

Back when everything happened, when I was first informing people, many of my friends who lived out of state declared that they would be making plans to come to California to support me and attend Erik's memorial, and I was so very appreciative for the offer, but the truth had been that I was already very supported by my family and Erik's family. I was afraid that if they came, I would feel bad if I wasn't able to spend the expected amount of time with them. By God's amazing grace, I had the foresight to ask that instead of coming to California, that they pick a weekend to come stay with me in St. Louis. God knew better than I did what I was in store for, and He made sure I was going to be taken care of.

For the first 6 months after everything happened, about every 2 to 4 weeks I had a friend or family member come to stay with me. I looked forward to every visit. It was always a wonderful distraction to have someone else in the house again, someone to sit on the front porch with. I could almost feel like the old me for a while. I got to be Kathy the friend, Kathy the aunt, Kathy the sister, or Kathy the niece and cousin. Kathy the widow was set in the corner, not out of view but out of the way for a bit.

Each visit was so special to me and helpful in some way. It was a time where I could get out of my own head and focus on something else, another person. And each visitor aided in my grief, showed me something I hadn't seen before, or introduced an idea I hadn't considered before. Some visitors were just a marvelous distraction which allowed me to laugh and reminisce and enjoy their company. Some were deep and meaningful.

But it never failed, as soon as my visitor backed out of the driveway after the weekend was over, it was back to reality, and a heaviness would fall on me like a bucket of tar and it made me feel ugly. No matter what I did, it accompanied me. When I went out, I thought for sure people would be able to see it on me. How could they not see it? But everywhere I went, people looked right past me, like nothing was wrong. At first I hadn't wanted anyone to notice, but then when they didn't, it created a deep loneliness inside me.

One day while I was running errands, I bumped into a woman that I worked with occasionally. We weren't friendly enough that I would have informed her of Erik's passing, but I knew she knew other people who already knew about Erik. When she saw me, she asked in a very congenial tone, "Hi Kathy! How are you?"

Panic struck me. *Does she know? She could know. But what if she doesn't know, should I say something? Or do I just pretend to be totally fine? But if she knows, then I appear cold and callous.* Inside, I was desperately wishing that if she did know, she would just come out with it and say something like, "I heard what happened and I'm so sorry." At least then I would know how to answer her. Finally, I gave her an "I'm good!" and made an excuse about being in a hurry.

I've always been a planner, finding comfort in mapping out the future. Yet, faced with an uncertain horizon, my mind drew blanks. The door to my future opened to a white wall of nothing. I couldn't even *imagine* what would happen next, and it started driving me crazy. Finally, I decided I had to stop. I realized that I would have to live solely in the present. I began the practice of every time my thoughts crept out of the boundary of the present day, I would corral them back in. On the hardest days, I had to really lasso them in closer. I would tell myself, *the future will be what it will be. Right now, this instant, is all that matters. How are you right now? I'm fine, I'm good,* would usually be the answer I gave myself, and I could move on with my day.

And that's how it went for the next 8 months.

I tried to find activities to occupy my time until I felt capable of working again. One activity was going through all the albums and boxes of pictures that Erik and I had accumulated of our life together and creating scrap books for Tosha, Tyler, and myself. It was wonderful and cathartic, chronicling our memories and organizing them into a timeline. The photos brought back so many happy memories and filled me with gratitude and kept sadness at bay.

In the mornings and evenings, I enjoyed walking Kira around our new neighborhood. In fact, Kira became my new best friend. I know I told Erik she was his dog, but there was no denying that she was always meant to be mine. God knew what was coming and He knew that I would need her. Every night I would go into the bedroom and read before going to sleep. Every night she would jump on the bed and lay down next to me. I would rest my hand on her side, feeling the comfort of having another living being next to me. She wouldn't budge an inch the whole time, not even when I put the book away and slid down into the covers. But as soon as I turned the light out, that was her cue to jump down and station herself at the front door, ready to prevent any intruder, allowing me to sleep peacefully.

During one of my evening strolls with Kira, another neighbor of mine was on her lawn and approached me as I neared her driveway. She introduced herself as Karen and she gave me her condolences. That small act of kindness sparked a friendship. She was a bit older than me, an OR nurse, divorced, and her 20-year-old son lived with her while he attended the community college. She was a lovely woman, scarred by divorce but content with her life. She was extremely busy, as are all nurses these days, and so we didn't have a lot of time together, but every few weeks we would enjoy a meal together, providing a much-needed respite from my solitude.

Emerging From the Dark

In August I finally felt capable of working again, of being able to concentrate again. I was a bit apprehensive at first, but my brain and fingers knew exactly what they had to do and it only took a few minutes for everything to start clicking again. The hardest part was after the deposition ended and my first thought was to call Erik to let him know I was done and heading home. It made my heart feel heavy and the drive home was melancholy.

There was sort of an odd coincidence that occurred on our street. My next-door neighbor, Ruby, lost her husband of 63 years just weeks after I lost Erik. Bob had been a very sweet 89-year-old World War II vet who enjoyed feeding Kira milk bones from his side of the fence. Kira got so accustomed to Bob's bones that every time we let her out into the backyard, she ran straight for the chain-link fence that separated our yards to wait for a visit from Bob.

On the other side of me, two houses down, Paul, a spry 90-year-old, lost his wife of 65 years.

Paul seemed to be struggling a bit with his loss. It was obvious he longed for company. Whenever he drove by and I was sitting on the front porch, he would pull into the driveway and come sit with me for a while. He was a hopeless flirt, and if I looked past his 90-year-old exterior, I could see a young handsome man still in there, a little cocky, but kind-hearted. Sometimes I would have to get after him and tell him to behave. He would say, "Oh, I'm harmless. I'm just nipping at the tires."

When Erik and I attended church in Missouri, we went to a church called The Crossing, a nondenominational church. It wasn't exactly a megachurch but it was akin. The building resembled more of a conference center than it did a church, complete with a cafeteria where you could purchase a coffee to enjoy during the service. Instead of pews, the church itself provided plush stadium seating. Prior to every service there was 30 minutes of contemporary Christian music performed by a band and singers. The large screen overhead displayed the words for people who wanted to sing along. It lacked the solemnity and reverence of Catholic churches, but the services were uplifting, and the pastor was an engaging speaker. However, in every sermon there would come a point that he would ask the congregants to contemplate a question with the people sitting next to you. If you were by yourself, you were supposed to join the people around you. This was so uncomfortable that I finally stopped going there in person and started viewing the services online instead.

I did, however, attempt to join a Bible study that the church was sponsoring. I went for the first night and I was assigned to a table of eight people. Everybody was cordial, but I didn't feel a friendship connection with anyone. I'm sure some of that could have been on me. I found it difficult to engage people like

I used to. I typically had no problem meeting people, asking about their work and family, things people love to talk about. My fear was that then the questions would come back to me. I didn't want to talk about me. This issue was taken care of for me because I got busy traveling with work again, and for many of the study evenings, I was out of town.

For my first birthday that year without Erik, I knew I wanted to go to Connecticut to visit Dawn and Glenda. Glenda was another of Tim's sisters that I was glad to have stayed friends with. After I moved away, she and I hadn't kept as close in contact as Dawn, but I would always consider her a good friend. No matter the time that has passed in between seeing each other, she is comfortable as family. We just pick up where we left off.

The Firsts

For my first birthday without Erik, I rented an Airbnb near Woodstock, New York, situated on a tranquil stream, surrounded by woods. Sharing it with Dawn, Glenda, their cousin Jen, who had been the first to learn about Erik, and then also Mark and Christy, the friends who saved me from Sharon, I couldn't think of a better way to start my 45th year.

It turned out to be a perfect September weekend for my birthday. I couldn't have picked better weather. You could feel the presence of fall on the horizon but everything was still very full and green. The running stream provided a background noise that was subtle and comforting. If you were enjoying conversation with another or deep in thought by yourself, you could miss it. But if you sat quietly and still, the sound filled your ears like a symphony, with the intermittent songs of different birds.

However, the best part of the weekend was reuniting with dear friends. Dawn, Glenda, and Jen surprised me with a spa day in Woodstock and also gifts and a cake. As Dawn sat next to me and I opened the gifts, a vision of Erik came to me. He was telling Dawn, "Take care of her for me." He and Dawn had formed a friendship throughout the years, mostly during our houseboat trips, and they enjoyed mutual respect. It is absolutely something he would have said to her. And that is exactly what she did.

After my amazing spa day, Mark and Christy joined us. We sat on the patio overlooking the stream and reminisced, sharing laughs and jokes. Mark has such a great sense of humor and it felt so good to laugh and be me again for a while. I was totally surrounded by the love of my friends, and I also felt the arms of God around me all weekend. I was filled with peace….about Erik, about my future. I could feel that somehow everything was going to be okay. And that was the best birthday gift ever.

Thanksgiving was spent with Erik's brother, Marshall, and his wife Mandy. Erik and I had been there the year before and I thought it would make me feel close to Erik to be in that familiar environment. Sadly, that wasn't what I experienced. And it was no fault of Marshall or Mandy or any of their guests, they were all very loving and supportive. The presence of Erik was too palpable. Instead of comforting me, as I anticipated, it rested heavy on my chest and made it hard to take a deep breath.

For Christmas that year, my sister Sherry, her husband Tom, my nephews Riley and Taylor and niece Haley all drove down from Minnesota to spend the holiday with me. They filled my home with warmth and hugs and laughs, just the things the house was missing. I was immensely grateful for each one of them. My sister has always been so gracious in sharing her kids with me that I feel so connected to each of them. They all have an enormous capacity for love, and for the whole time they were with me, I was engulfed in it. When it was time for them to go, we engaged in the typical Minnesota goodbye, standing by the car, hugging, and saying our farewells, and then sharing thoughts that somehow hadn't occurred to us in all the hours that we spent talking over the past three days, and then of course followed by another round of hugs and I-love-yous. Minnesota goodbyes are infamous for easily lasting up to an hour.

CHAPTER 6

The Courage To Start Over

The week between Christmas and New Year's is a reliably
slow week in the court reporting industry. Many attorneys
take that time off and trials are rarely set for that week. My list
of visitors and my plans for travel had all been spent. By the
third day, I had handed in all my outstanding transcripts, the
house was clean, the dishwasher was empty, and all the laundry
was folded and put away. I was completely bored. I decided to
surf the internet a bit. Something I very rarely had time for,
nor the inclination, but for some reason it sounded appealing at
that moment. *Let's see...where to start.* eHarmony came to mind,
thinking that someday in the future, WAY in the future, I may
venture out of my tent of grief and be ready to meet people.

I typed eHarmony into Google and quickly found a link
that I was expecting to provide information on pricing and
how it all works, but before it would allow me to access a
page with information, I had to click on "Start Free Today".
Okay, fine. That led to a page asking for my email address and
name. *Seriously? Just to find out how much it is?* Somewhat irked,
I entered my information. *I'll just unsubscribe once they start
bombarding me with emails.* Then there was another question,
and another question, and next thing I knew, it said, "You have

a profile!" *What?! Wait! No! I don't want a profile! I'm not ready for a profile!*

Then it said, "You've been matched with 3 matches in your area." And you could continue for free, but in order to see pictures, you were required to pay a small fee for a 3-month subscription.

Oh, come on! I sat there for a moment, and suddenly I was feeling that same feeling I had as I was driving to Colorado to meet Erik, like I was on the precipice of something potentially life-changing. *How could I meet someone so soon after losing Erik and not compare them to Erik? And what would people say if they knew I was doing this? It hasn't even been a year.* It also felt like I was cheating on Erik. It felt disrespectful to him. *But what if I just met someone I could go to a movie with. It could be a good distraction.*

As my mind argued with itself, I decided to step back, and I pushed the computer away from me. I bowed my head and closed my eyes. *God, what is this? Is this you? If this is not you, I don't want it. Please, please, guide me here.* I had that very deep sense again that this would be another defining moment in my life, and it was crucial that I make the right choice. I sat for a few more minutes in silence, just trying to quiet my mind and listen.

I've got nothing to lose but everything to gain.

"Well, all right, then." I said out loud, in submission to that voice.

Next thing I know, I'm looking at the pictures of the three gentlemen I was matched with. One immediately caught my eye. He was very handsome, for sure, but there was something about the way he smiled with his whole face, especially his eyes. There was an exuberance in those eyes. However, his profile also caught my attention. He was a chiropractor who loved healthy living as much as he loved Jesus. *Wowza.* That was definitely a combination that piqued my interest. I would later learn his name was Chris Heeb.

Throughout the rest of December and January, we exchanged a series of "winks" and auto generated questions for both of us, and our contact then escalated to emails. I had been right, this had been a wonderful distraction, but this next step filled me with excitement and sometimes unbearable guilt. As we exchanged emails about our personal lives, I found myself more and more looking forward to reading his emails. The emails were fun because I was able to hear his "voice" in our conversations and I got a flavor of who he was. In one email he described himself as "a good ol' Catholic boy who loves wine and loves Jesus."

However, there was one email that made me pause in my tracks. He told me he had two sets of twins, ages 10 and 18. I did a doubletake. Four kids and two of them were the age that Tosha was when I first met Erik. I knew I was starting over, but I hadn't considered starting all the way over.

Okay, God, you got me here. This is not what I would have wished for. But I trust you and so I need to know if this is all part of your plan for me.

And it didn't take long to receive an answer. If this is who God wants for me, then there is purpose for them in my life and purpose for me in their lives.

The next logical step was to meet. We picked a time on a Monday evening to meet at a mutually convenient Starbucks. It was February 1st and we had been having a cold spell. I bundled up in a black turtleneck sweater, jeans, and warm black boots. On the drive over I was once again pondering the possible outcomes of this meeting. *What am I doing? This is craziness.* The difference between this encounter and the one with Erik was I knew what Chris looked like. If Erik was Mel Gibson, Chris was George Clooney. *What the heck. What have I got to lose. At the very least I had a good distraction for a while.*

I parked the car and my stomach did flipflops like a school girl on her first date. However, after everything that had happened and the way I had felt the last 8 months, this feeling of excitement was a welcome respite from the grieving process. It was fun. Even if nothing came of it, it gave me a much-appreciated break.

Chris had texted me while I was pulling up and parking, "I'm here." *Oh, man. Here we go.*

I opened the door to Starbucks and saw him instantly. He had on a long black winter coat, blue jeans, and a button-down shirt. He was every bit as handsome as his photos. He saw me right away and came over to me, greeting me warmly with a smile and giving me a kiss on the cheek as we shook hands. The minute he pulled away and I looked in his eyes, my very first thought was, *this man is going to be my husband.* No doubt whatsoever. None. I knew it like I knew my name. After we exchanged pleasantries and ordered our beverages, I excused myself to use the ladies room and I just started laughing as I looked in the mirror. *Holy cow, God. You are unbelievable.*

We spent the rest of the evening sipping tea at Starbucks and talking. The whole time Chris was talking, I had to fight the urge to put my hand on his knee or touch his arm. He was just so familiar to me that it felt like a natural thing to do, but I had to keep reminding myself that Chris had probably not been privy to the same message I had been.

When Starbucks started closing up, we found a tavern next door and continued our conversation, except we switched to water instead of tea. Neither of us was interested in getting anything stronger. I was so distracted by my own thoughts at times that I barely heard what he was saying. *I really can't believe this. This is so crazy.* Finally, the tavern kicked us out and since it was late, we concluded it was best to call it a night.

As Chris and I stood by my car, we couldn't stop smiling at each other. I wanted to memorize this moment, how he looked, because I knew that this was a memory that I would want to replay for the rest of my life, the day that Chris Heeb came into my world.

The whole drive home my mind whirred with frantic thoughts, *God, what are you doing? You just never cease to surprise me.* It reminded me that God is God and He can do anything, and He did it again!

A month after our Starbucks encounter, I found myself sitting down to write Chris a letter. The words flowed effortlessly from my pen onto the legal pad, filling 10 pages without pause. When I finished, I exhaled deeply, recognizing the gravity of what I had just written. I folded it and sealed it in an envelope. I placed the envelope in my desk drawer with the plan that he would receive it on our wedding night. As I tried to reflect on my words, I was surprised that the contents were no longer stored in my memory.

Becoming a Grandmother

Barely a month after meeting Chris, I flew to Italy with Tosha's mother, Shawna. Tosha had given birth to twins, and she and Kevin were looking forward to some help, Shawna and I were looking forward to meeting our first grandchildren.

It was a bittersweet occasion, meeting little Adee and Tristan for the first time. I was filled with so much love and joy for the twins and for Tosha and Kevin, after all they went through to get pregnant, finally succeeding with IVF, in vitro fertilization. At the same time, I felt immense sadness that Erik wasn't there to share in it. Especially since Erik loved to be around babies. Of the two of us, if somebody asked if we wanted to hold their new baby, I would be the first to say, "No, thanks. I'm good." Whereas Erik would reach his arms out before they could barely complete their question.

Being there with the twins felt different for me though. I loved them so much and I wanted to love them for Erik too.

Shawna and I spent most of our time helping with feeding the twins, preparing meals, or keeping up with laundry, but we also had some days out to explore Sicily, which is where they were stationed. One memorable day, Kevin and I embarked on a wine tasting adventure at the Donnafugata winery in Marsala and explored the historic town of Erice. Kevin proved to be a delightful and knowledgeable tour guide, and the day was filled with engaging conversation and plenty of laughter.

Reflecting on Tosha and Kevin's journey, I couldn't help but marvel at their enduring marriage. When they first started dating, we liked Kevin, but we were more than a little skeptical when they announced that Kevin was joining the Navy and they were planning to marry before he left for boot camp, which was just a few months away. They were 20 years old, still kids in our minds. How could this work? They would marry and then he would leave? Erik was raised in a military family and saw firsthand the struggles it produced. We were concerned, to say the least.

But Tosha and Kevin proved us wrong. Today, their marriage is as strong as ever and they just celebrated 14 years. Through the years, I have been in awe, witnessing their struggles and how they always are finding ways to overcome them.

Two years ago they sold their house and bought a brand-new fifth wheel camper and truck to pull it. They decided to forego material items and focus more on experiences. Now they spend most of their time outdoors and exploring new areas.

To watch Tosha grow from an awkward 10-year-old to this beautiful, mature, loving woman, knowing the struggles of her youth and teen years, I am filled with admiration. At every turn where her life could have gone down a dark path, she chose the opposite no matter how difficult it was, even if it meant stepping out of her comfort zone, learning more about herself, and realizing truths about her family. Tosha set out on a pursuit to make a happy life for herself, her husband, and her children, and that's exactly what she did. Not a perfect life, but a joyful and fulfilling life. Every time we speak, I feel I have so much to learn from her.

Finding Love Again

Upon returning from Italy, Chris and I then began the journey of our courtship, learning each other's likes, dislikes, food preferences and food aversions. We became familiar with different moods and cues. We presented our best selves until our worst cleverly snuck out without permission, and we decided that even the other's worst parts were acceptable.

One aspect I discovered about Chris was his passion for cooking, which was evident in every meal he prepared. Whether crafting a simple breakfast sandwich or an elaborate dish like filet mignon stuffed with crab meat, Chris throws in a touch of this or splash of that to send your senses into a whole new realm of delight. While I may not contribute much in the kitchen, I relish the opportunity to share a glass of wine and observe his culinary prowess. He loves to pair the meal with the right wine, just like he pairs the right music with what he's cooking. Often in between timers buzzing, he will invite me into his arms and we will slow dance around the kitchen to an old 1970s song playing on Yacht Rock radio, with rich aromas of the meal surrounding us.

His energy and passion in the kitchen and for food is the same for growing flowers and herbs. As soon as the weather makes the switch from winter to spring, Chris is prepping his pots, organizing his seeds, and deciding which ones to plant. Then begin the trips to Home Depot to view the discount rack of plants. The joy he receives from bringing half dead plants back to life makes my heart smile.

As our relationship deepened, I found myself plagued by dreams of Erik. In every dream, he was still alive, making me choose between him and Chris. At first it was tormenting, and I felt so conflicted. I wanted to choose Chris but the guilt was overwhelming. I would wake up with a knot in my stomach, unsettled, feeling like I was cheating on my husband.

As time passed and our relationship progressed, the dreams became less frequent, less agonizing. In one dream, Erik appeared but he didn't speak, yet I knew he was expecting me to choose.

With great sadness and sincerity, I said to him, "Honey, I'm sorry, you've been gone too long."

The last dream of this type I was finally able to tell him that I was with Chris now. I again explained to Erik that he had been gone too long. In that dream, Erik didn't get angry, again he didn't speak, he just faded away, and that was the end of those dreams. The guilt I was harboring dissipated as well.

Towards the autumn season of our relationship, literally and figuratively, I felt that Chris was beginning to pull back. It was hurtful and I went into protection mode and pulled back myself. Doubts started to form in my head. *Had I been wrong about God's message? Was my grief making me imagine things? Or maybe I'm just going crazy.*

A few days passed and I received a card in my mailbox. It was apparent by the absence of a stamp that it had been hand-delivered. When I opened the card, there was a folded piece of white printer paper. When I unfolded it, there was a list of 10 numbered items with the heading "Things I Demand For My Next Wife."

As I read down the list, I mentally put a checkmark next to each item. Of course, some of the items described the usual qualities you would look for in a spouse. The items that really caught my attention were:

1. No kids.

2. Must be Catholic.

Suddenly my whole life made sense.

Throughout my life, I've often felt like a freak of nature because I never harbored the desire to have children. I have known this about me since high school, when friends were starting to talk about their futures, going to school, getting jobs, getting married, and having kids. Whenever the subject of having kids was raised, it immediately repelled me. That wasn't to say that I didn't like children. I adored my sister's four little munchkins. I even moved across the country to be a nanny. And Erik's daughter and son became treasured stepchildren. The only thing I could deduce from this dichotomy is that I love *other people's* children.

During my time with Tim, I occasionally attended Catholic Masses with him, despite being raised Presbyterian. I enjoyed the tradition and solemness of the Catholic faith, but I never contemplated conversion until an enlightening experience at an Emmaus retreat. It was there that God's presence became undeniably clear to me, guiding my path towards Catholicism, and in doing so, guiding me towards Chris. God had placed on Chris's heart that he not deviate from his list of demands, and upon meeting me, Chris felt certain I was the person his list had been inspired by.

That was a pivotal point for us. Just when I thought I had horribly misinterpreted another message or imagined it altogether, God prompted Chris to reach out, which helped me to hold on a little longer.

As Chris and I continued to get closer and started planning a future together, it bothered me a bit that although we were coming up on a year together, I still hadn't met his children. I calmed the nagging by reminding myself that I respected his decision to wait to see where our relationship was heading. It was good parenting. After his previous live-in girlfriend of six years moved out, it had been difficult for the younger twins, especially because they had been sharing their childhood with her daughter. However, I saw this as a sign that Chris was obviously not as sure about our relationship as I was.

One afternoon shortly before Christmas, as Chris was sitting at my kitchen table and I was making us some tea, Chris said nonchalantly, "So I was thinking, I'll be with my kids for Christmas Eve, but then Christmas Day, I thought we could go to my sister's. She's having everyone over."

Maybe it was the head cold I happened to be suffering with, but tears sprung to my eyes before I could order them back. My voice was raspy and barely audible because of my cold and also because I knew the response to what I was about to say could impact the rest of my life.

"If I had thought I was going to be alone on Christmas Eve, I would have gone home to Minnesota," I said. It was at that moment that I knew I had to put Chris to the test, and I had to put my premonition to the test.

"Chris, if you don't know by now about us, I'd rather be heartbroken now than three years from now."

Chris's eyes began to glisten by seeing my tears. "You'll be with me and my kids on Christmas Eve."

"Are you sure?"

"Yes. I'm positive."

Before he left to pick up his boys from school, he dried my tears and quelled my fears. As he drove away, my heart was dancing and I am sure I had a huge silly smile on my face, the same as when we first met. Within 30 minutes of his departure, he was back ringing my doorbell. When I answered, he handed me a plastic bag with different cold remedies. It was so sweet, I kissed him right there on the doorstep.

"My boys are in the car," he said through a big grin.

"Oh, no! I'm so sorry!" I hadn't even thought of them.

"It's okay, I already told them about you."

As I looked over to the car, two adorable little boys gave me big toothy smiles and a friendly wave.

And that's when I knew I had been right. I had read the message from God correctly this time. My heart was overflowing with gratitude.

As Christmas Eve approached, however, I felt very cognizant of the fact that I was now, in a sense, "The Other Woman." To his kids, I was the woman who wasn't their mother being thrust into their lives. I was curious and a bit nervous about how the older twins, Holly and Dillon, would accept me. I was familiar with the younger twins, Chase and Preston, because I had met them casually before, but this would be the first time meeting Holly and Dillon, and on Christmas Eve, no less. I felt like I was intruding on a day they should have had their dad to themselves. I'm regretful to say it was purely selfish on my part, I didn't want to be alone on Christmas Eve. Had I to do it over again, I would have picked another day to meet them. And it's not because they weren't kind to me, they were extremely polite, much nicer than I had been when I was in their situation, but there was some awkwardness for sure, and I take full responsibility for that. I knew better.

In the eight years since then, it astounds me how fortunate I was to find another family that accepted me so warmly. I feel like I hit the jackpot twice, first with Erik's kids and now with Chris's. Holly, Dillon, Chase, and Preston are just simply amazing human beings. They are respectful to us, and they are also just as respectful to each other. They encourage each other, tease each other, and laugh together. Through the years, we have taken road trips and vacations together, shared holidays and major milestones in their lives, and I've treasured and enjoyed every minute.

When the lease expired for the house I was renting, Chris and I embarked on a new chapter, a fresh start for each of us, in Kirkwood, a charming suburb of St. Louis with hundred-year-old houses and quaint restaurants. It was large enough for Chris and me, as well as his two younger boys and our dogs, Kira and Chris's dog Stephi, a Lab and Bernese Mountain Dog mix.

On the last day of packing up my house and boxing everything up, I sat on the porch alone for the last time, waiting for the movers. I grabbed my journal and a pen and I sat down with my thoughts.

"Today I am sitting on the front porch of this house on Bridgeport Drive for the last time. I have Kira at my feet and it's a beautiful day – just a little cool, but it feels good after lugging everything from the basement into the garage. I must have made 50 trips up and down the stairs, or at least it felt like it.

"Next week I move into the first home that Chris and I will share as husband and wife. We have set the date for July 2nd. I cannot even put into words how happy he makes me. What a gift from God he is. Yet, as I sit on this porch for the last time, the last porch that Erik and I sat on together, I can't help but feel a little bit sad. Another piece of Erik slips away, or, more accurately, I'm walking away from.

"I have to remind myself that it doesn't matter that I don't display his pictures or that I sold his favorite chair, those things are not Erik. Erik will live in my heart forever. I have 16 years of memories that I will always have.

"I have absolutely no doubt that I am ready to embark on a new adventure with Chris, and I have absolutely no doubt that he is the one God chose for me. But I am giving myself this moment and I am giving it to Erik, because when I leave here, my new life begins, and Chris deserves to have all of my heart and I want him to have it. Erik will forever be a part of me, but he will have to be in the quiet part of my soul. The rest belongs to Chris now and I can't wait to see what this new chapter has in store for me."

On July 2, 2016, in Sanibel, Florida, the morning after Chris and I said our vows on the beach at sunset, we sat in the living room with booming thunder clouds and bright lightning flashes in the background, and Chris read the letter that I had written all those months ago, the letter that started out, "You don't know this yet, but some day you're going to love me."

This is what God can do when we get out of the way. When I couldn't see a future and I handed it over to God, He turned it into more than I could have ever thought to ask for and He gave me the courage to accept it.

Thank you, God, for your guidance and direction and for putting Chris in my life. Thank you for the courage to heed your plans for my life and not what others' expectations of me might be.

Mom, Dad, Brad, Sherry

Brad, Sherry

Hartjes and Andersons 2021

Taffy

Dad, me 1999

Red Rock Retreat

Tyler, me, Tosha 201

Erik, me,
Tosha, Tyler 1999

Erik, me,
Majesty, Taffy 1998

JR, Erik 6/17/1

The Bauernfeinds 2014

Jen, Dawn, me, Glenda

Christy, me, Mark

Me, Mom #2

Chandra, me

Me, Robin

Christy, Babs, me

my, Jody, Lorna, Lori, me

Kira, Me

Sanibel Island, FL, 2016

The Heebs 2022

Chris, me, 2022

The Heebs 2018

Chris, me, 2019

Tosha's family 2022

CHAPTER 7

Be Your Own Best Friend

Seven months post diagnosis, and as mobility has gotten more and more challenging, I have had to find new ways to do practically everything. Walking is only done with a walker. If I need to get into a space that doesn't allow for the walker, such as our closet or our laundry room, I have to hold on to other things for support. Showering requires a shower chair and a lot of energy.

Standing up from the couch requires holding on to our coffee table and the sofa arm and pushing myself up. Frequently it takes more than one try, especially if I don't have a lot of energy that day. It starts with taking a long, deep breath. I have to prepare myself mentally. *Okay. I can do this.* Then before I attempt it, I envision myself standing. Another deep breath. I place one hand on the coffee table, one hand on the arm of the sofa, and I push off. Oftentimes that first try I'm barely able to lift my bottom off the couch. *It's okay. Just take a deep breath. You can do this.*

I try again and I concentrate on my upper thigh area in an effort to straighten my legs and then use my upper arm strength to push me off the sofa. Once I get my legs straight, I'm still bent over and holding myself up by my arms. I'm using every ounce of strength in my arms to keep me standing, but now I have to move one arm to my walker. *Keep your legs straight, strong. You got this. You can do this.* And then I take a leap of faith that, as I move my hand from the coffee table to the walker, that my legs will hold up. Once I have one hand on my walker, the other follows much easier. And that is what I endure every single time I have to stand up. From anywhere.

I have come to learn that many times the difference between my being able to stand or not is largely dependent on what I tell myself. When I attempt to stand and it doesn't work, my mind immediately wants to think *I can't do it.* And if that's what I'm thinking when I try again, I'm right. I can't. That's when I take a pause, a deep breath, and adjust my thinking. *I can do this.* So far, my legs respond positively to the declaration, and they cooperate.

The Bible has told us in Proverbs 15:4, "Gentle words bring life and health; a deceitful tongue crushes the spirit."

And 16:24, "Kind words are like honey – sweet to the soul and healthy for the body."

I believe these verses apply to how we speak to ourselves as well as other people. "Gentle words bring life and health." "Kind words are….healthy for the body." How many times have your own thoughts made you feel worthless or stupid, even sick? For me, too many to count.

Not long after being diagnosed with breast cancer in 2020, a friend of ours recommended a book to me called "The Untethered Soul: The Journey Beyond Yourself" written by Michael Alan Singer. There is an exercise in the book where it asks you to listen to how you talk to yourself. To do this, you sit quietly and comfortably. Close your eyes. Pretend that the voice you hear in your head is actually sitting next to you. What are they saying? How are they saying it? I practiced this a few times and it was interesting to me but, apparently, I didn't have a whole lot to say to myself at those moments. However, it did make me more aware throughout the day of that voice in my head.

The day that my inner voice was legitimately revealed was a day when I was in our master bathroom, having an emotional moment from all the worry and stress that comes with a breast cancer diagnosis, and I started to cry. I looked in the mirror and narrowed my eyes and I said to myself, *Listen here you Sally crybaby, you gotta get it together.*

I instantly stepped back from the mirror. *Sally crybaby? Where did that come from?* I couldn't remember hearing that anywhere. And why was my inner voice such a jerk? I had every right to have an emotional moment if I wanted to. What if somebody else had said that to me? I would have told them to pound sand. Completely unacceptable. That's when I knew I needed to replace the jerk in my head with a friendly voice. When enduring a difficult time in your life, the last thing you need is a big fat bully hanging out in your head. From then on, I vowed that whenever I would catch the tyrant coming out, I would ask myself, *is that something I would say to a friend?*

It took several attempts to find a voice I was comfortable with. I started to notice when walking and daily activities started to become challenging, that a drill sergeant started taking residence, barking at me: *Stand up! Do it now! Failing is not an option!* Eventually I was able to tame it down to a personal trainer: *No rests! Give me 10 more steps! You got this!* But now that voice is more of an occupational therapist: *Okay, Kathy, you're doing great. It's okay to take a break. Deep breath and try again.*

There are also times when the voice is that of a dear friend. That voice is always there for me when I start to feel down or scared. *It's okay to feel this way. Stay close to God. Trust God. He will get you through this. You're doing great. Just focus on today, right now. Give Jesus your future.*

What a difference a day is when you're on your own side. Some days it's easy to be my own cheerleader, and then other days I have to work really hard at it, which are usually the days that I didn't sleep well and I'm tired, the days that I'm worn out physically and mentally and I just want to take a day off of suffering. But suffering doesn't allow for days off. No rest for the weary, as they say. Those days require more patience, more gratitude, and more compassion towards myself. That's when I am constantly reminding myself, this is temporary, my circumstances will change, and God is God and He can do anything. In the meantime, be kind to yourself.

CHAPTER 8

Let It Go

I am of the belief that cancer, at least for some, is an expression of imbalance somewhere in your life. For some, it's diet. For others, it's obesity, perhaps it's lifestyle. According to those criteria, I appeared to be the epitome of someone who should not develop cancer: maintaining a healthy weight, adhering to a balanced diet, abstaining from smoking and excessive drinking, and lacking a family history of breast cancer. Consequently, when I received my first diagnosis of breast cancer in 2020, I couldn't help but speculate on potential psychological factors. Following Erik's passing, I delved into literature that suggested cancer could arise after a traumatic event, typically surfacing 6 to 8 years afterward. Although I believed I had grieved sufficiently, I couldn't shake the notion that perhaps there were lingering unresolved emotions contributing to my illness.

I also grappled with the possibility of harboring unresolved feelings toward my mother. Despite forgiving her for any past transgressions, a lingering sense of unease persisted. While I reassured myself that she and I were reconciled before she left this earth, a latent anger occasionally surfaced, without any perceived trigger or target. It was possible it had nothing to do with my mother. It would usually come at night when I was trying to sleep, but it could even find me on my yoga mat during a savasana. Something would pop into my head and once it was there, it would start as a lit match and quickly become a forest fire. It would make me sick to my stomach, I would get so angry. And it could stem from something extremely minor, things that did not warrant such an intense response. Many times, the anger was directed at me. Like when tax season came around, I would chastise myself for not saving money for my estimated payments. *Kathy, how could you be so stupid again. You do this every year! Why do you do this to yourself. You need to make time for this...*and on and on and on until I was sick to my stomach.

After my diagnosis of breast cancer, I resolved to explore the possibility that this was somehow affecting my health. Unfortunately, in May of 2020 we were in the midst of the mandatory lockdown due to COVID. There were no therapists that were seeing patients in person. Despite the availability of remote consultations, I hesitated, feeling uncomfortable with such arrangements. Thus, I postponed this pursuit, redirecting my focus toward other health-promoting endeavors.

Upon being diagnosed with terminal cancer, I knew I couldn't ignore the fact that I had never revisited the idea of seeking counseling for any psychological baggage I might be carrying. Now that COVID was in the rearview, I had no excuses.

Chris recommended the counselor that he had been seeing off and on for many years. She was good at bringing things to light that he hadn't considered or recognized about himself, others, or a situation he was struggling with. I made an appointment with her and looked forward to meeting her.

I was not surprised when I met her that she was exactly what I had pictured when Chris had told me about her. She was in her mid-40s perhaps but looked younger than her age. Dressed nicely but not flashy, in a skirt that went to her knees and a cardigan sweater. She had shoulder length dirty blond hair and thin build, and she spoke with a kind voice and understanding eyes. I could see why Chris felt so comfortable around her. She reminded me of a cross between my second grade schoolteacher and Dawn.

The first session with Mary Beth was mostly her getting to know a brief synopsis of my background, my family, an overview of my life. We chatted briefly about my late husband, Erik. Towards the end of the session, she recommended a book called "No Bad Parts" by Richard Schwartz. The book describes how we each have many different parts inside us. It's why we may act differently when we are with different people or in different situations. The way you act or talk at the office may be different than how you act or speak at home or with your friends. Some of these parts are from childhood, and they have lingered, sometimes causing pain to our present self without even realizing it. The book was very illuminating to me.

On our second session, we talked about the book and what I thought about it and the role that my mother possibly played in some of the anger I would feel. Mary Beth introduced me to Eye Movement Desensitization and Reprocessing (EMDR), designed to address trauma or other distressing life experiences.

The therapy started with me sitting directly across from Mary Beth, both feet on the floor. She handed me two rubber balls, one for each hand. The balls were attached to a device that she held in her hands. She asked me to close my eyes and to just be quiet and explained that the balls were going to vibrate intermittently, from one hand to the other. I was to scan my body and notice any pains or sources of discomfort. After a few minutes, I felt a pang in my stomach area and so I decided to focus on that.

She requested that I speak to that area in my mind, ask it why it's there. We sat for several minutes in quiet while I waited for some kind of response from my pain. When my mind began to wander, I would gently bring it back to that area. After about 10 minutes, the pang I had felt earlier repeated itself. But in that instant of pain, an image appeared in my head. It was the face of an angry man with a snarled face and raised fists, as if trying to break through my stomach. And as quickly as it showed itself, it was gone. *Whoa. What was THAT?*

After a few more minutes of sitting silently, I waited for the face to reappear, but it did not. When the exercise was over, Mary Beth asked me, "Did you see anything?"

I shared with her the image that I saw. I could still see it in my mind. "It reminded me of the anger I get sometimes," and I described it as best I could.

"When is the first time you remember feeling that anger?" She asked me.

I contemplated the question. "It was when my dad left when I was 15."

"Picture that 15-year-old you. Tell her it's okay. She's going to be okay."

The minute she said that and I pictured myself back at that time, the tears began to flow. I could see her (me), trying so hard not to care about my dad leaving because caring hurt too much. I could feel her frustration, her pain, and her guilt. I knew in that moment that this is where we would need to start in order for me to heal.

The next day, when I was sharing my experience with Dawn about the angry man with the fists, she asked me, "Did you think you could talk to it?"

I pondered the question and thought back to the image. "No, it was gone too quickly. Almost like it had been hiding and didn't mean to show itself."

After my conversation with Dawn and the insight she had drawn from me, I kept thinking of my 15-year-old self and that angry face trying not to be seen. Suddenly the memories and feelings came flooding back.

Birthday Surprise

Minnesota, fall 1985: For my 16th birthday, to my surprise and delight, my dad offered to take me shopping for my gift. I was slightly excited about the gift but more so to spend time with him. Since he had left the house, I hadn't seen much of him.

He picked me up on a Saturday morning, and I was all smiles with anticipation for our day. In my mind I was thinking maybe after shopping we would get lunch or go bowling. I would have agreed to just about anything if it meant spending the whole day with him.

As we started to drive, my dad brought up casually, "We're going to stop and pick up a friend to come with us." *A friend? Why would one of dad's friends come with us?*

"Who is it?" I asked naively.

"Just a friend from work." *That's weird, but okay.* It didn't faze my good mood at all.

I still wasn't thinking much about it when we pulled up to the condo complex and walked up to the door. I was with my dad and my heart was light and happy. Dad knocked on the door and we waited. When the door opened, my stomach did a turn and my smile disappeared. Since when did dad become friends with women who wore stylish clothes and wore makeup and had short chic haircuts, who, I also noted, were clearly much younger than him?

She smiled a big smile, and as we entered her condominium, my dad gave her a kiss on the cheek. Happy birthday to me, here's a big fat punch to the gut.

I learned that her name was Sonia and she did in fact work with my dad at the Elks Club. He had been a bookkeeper there for a number of years and she worked in the office. As I stood awkwardly in her living room, I couldn't help but feel so out of place around this modern 1980s mauve décor that looked and felt nothing like our home. And the way dad was acting I had never seen before. He was almost giggly and looking all googly-eyed at her. As much as I didn't like my mom, it angered me that I had never seen him act that way with mom, HIS WIFE. This Sonia woman was also way too modern with her high-waisted designer jeans and printed shirt. The more she smiled and tried to engage me in conversation, the more I hated her.

As we drove to the mall, I naturally got sent to the backseat, both literally and figuratively. Clearly this whole charade of a shopping day for me, to celebrate my birthday, was more about dad showing off his new puppy. *Dad, I thought you said there hadn't been another woman. What the hell is this? I'm not stupid.*

We arrived at the mall and I decided I wanted a boom box for my birthday. This was 1985 and they were all the rage. You could carry them around and you could also record music from the radio onto a cassette. Yep, dad was going to pay for this with a big fat blow to his pocketbook.

As we walked through the mall, I thought I would vomit when I saw my dad and this woman holding hands. *Are you kidding me? Who is this man that used to be my dad? I have no idea who this guy is. You know who would have loved to hold your hand, dad? Mom, that's who!*

I couldn't even walk next to them. I quickened my pace and walked in front of them so that I didn't have to look at them. We walked into the electronics store and I went straight to the stereo section and I pointed at the largest boom box I could find. "I want that one." I knew it was expensive and I didn't care. I also knew he wouldn't say no in front of his little hotsy-totsy.

I didn't say a word on the way home. There was no lunch and there was no bowling and no time with my dad that I had been wanting and needing so badly. *They* had plans and so they took me home. I felt like an abandoned dog as they drove away. *What just happened? How could dad do this?* I was trying to reconcile in my barely 16-year-old head the dad that I grew up worshipping and this dad who gave this other woman all the laughs and "sweeties" that should have been mine.

I went into my room with my new boom box and I didn't even take it out of the box. I was still feeling sick to my stomach. I felt betrayed, like he had cheated on *me*, not just my mother. Yet, at the same time, I didn't *want* to feel that way. Because then it would be like I didn't have a dad anymore, I wouldn't have *my* dad anymore, the dad that taught me how to ride my bike and drive a car and called me Taffy Dawn.

Bringing back these memories made me realize that it was then that I decided to tuck this anger away.

Who cares. I don't care. I don't care. Don't think about it. And I told myself that enough times that I believed it. From that point on, every time dad disappointed me, I didn't care and I didn't think about it.

As soon as I acknowledged that this is where that deep anger stemmed from, it lifted a weight I hadn't even realized I was carrying. I pictured my 16-year-old-self trying so hard to keep the image of her father intact, pushing that anger down and not allowing it to be expressed, not mature enough yet to understand that our parents have faults, they're not perfect, and that they were just doing the best they could. As an adult I could forgive my dad for his shortcomings and still love him for all that he had been to me.

I don't think I got cancer because of the repressed anger, but I know that the moment I let go of it, I felt a burden rise out of me and I immediately felt lighter. So far it has not returned. And it occurs to me that had it not been for this diagnosis, I would still be harboring that anger, that pain.

Thank you, God, for this cancer and for helping me to let this go. Thank you for healing my heart.

CHAPTER 9

Choose Wisely
The Voice You Listen To

The first time my doctor brought up hospice to me, I thought nothing of it. It was 3 months into my diagnosis and so it seemed like a natural and inevitable topic that needed to be discussed.

"I know you don't need it now, but when you're ready, we can talk about hospice. I can help get that set up for you and so you'll be comfortable," she had said.

My primary care doctor is in her early 40s with a thin build and sharp features, her shoulder length straight brown hair parted in the middle and tucked behind her ears. I have nicknamed her as Dr. Doom.

At the time, I was still walking on my own for short distances, or I held onto an arm if I had someone near me. No walker, no wheelchair. I was still working and still feeling good except for back pain that was developing. I had reached out to Dr. Doom to see if she could prescribe something for the discomfort.

The second time she brought up hospice, I was 5 months into my diagnosis. By then, I had just started using a walker, mainly for balance. I was still feeling good, still working, still enjoying life. I had called because there had been an issue with the pharmacy filling my prescription for the gabapentin she had prescribed.

"How are you doing?" Dr. Doom asked me, with a sympathetic tone indicative of anticipating an answer of pain and suffering.

"I'm good!"

We chatted briefly about the reason for my call and she said again, "It doesn't sound like you're ready now, but when you are, we can get hospice set up for you."

Why does she keep bringing that up? Like I could forget?

"Um, I'm good right now."

"It's been a while since I've seen you. Why don't you come in. I'd like to see you and get some blood work done," she said, sounding a bit curious as to why I wasn't doom and gloom.

We made an appointment for the following week, and Chris accompanied me into the exam room. We sat down in chairs next to the desk that we presumed Dr. Doom would be sitting at. Within a few minutes, she entered the room and we smiled and said hello.

Dr. Doom looked at me, seeming a bit surprised, "You look really good," she remarked.

"Thanks! I feel pretty good!"

After she performed some simple strength tests on my arms and legs, she told me, "Your strength is good."

She sat back on her stool and opened my medical file. "How is the gabapentin working?" she asked as she scanned the file.

"Actually, it's giving me some side aches and tightness in my torso. I was wondering if we could change it?"

"There's another drug that's similar but may not have the side effects. It's Lyrica, or the generic is pregabalin. We can try that."

"That sounds great."

"Otherwise, how are you feeling?" Again, the sympathetic tone. Had she not heard me before?

"I'm good!"

"Well, you know how this is going to end, so when you're ready for hospice, you can just let us know. You don't have to try to be strong and suffer through it."

Are you kidding me? What do I even say to that?

"Yeah, I know," was all I could think of.

"I know you're not ready now, but when you are, whether it's weeks or months from now."

"Or ever." I smiled. She just gave me another sympathetic smile.

What Dr. Doom didn't know was that as soon as I got over the initial shock of my diagnosis, I remembered that nobody knows my expiration date except God. I made a vow to myself that I would just live each day with gratitude and let God worry about the rest. I don't think Dr. Doom knows that God is God and He can do anything.

As Chris and I were walking to the car, I could tell he was upset. When we got in, he couldn't contain it. "That was absolutely ridiculous. Hospice? Really? The only thing out of her mouth should have been, 'You look great. Keep doing what you're doing.' That's it!"

Up to this point it didn't really bother me. I attributed her behavior to being young and being a doctor. She probably hadn't seen anybody with a terminal diagnosis survive before. I knew she wasn't trying to be mean or insensitive, she was doing her job. She was working off of statistics. And statistics say I will be needing hospice very shortly. But I guess I'm not a statistic.

The last time Dr. Doom brought up hospice to me was 8 months into my diagnosis. I had a video chat with her regarding some questions I had.

"How are you feeling?" in the same sympathetic tone.

"I'm good!" Which was true. I was still walking with the walker, still working, and still enjoying life. Chris and I were still getting together with friends and we also attended the St. Louis Symphony frequently.

"Well, I know you're not ready yet, but just let me know when we can get hospice set up for you."

"Dr. Doom, don't you think I'm doing really well so far?"

"Well, you know, you were really healthy to start with and everybody is different." It wasn't so much what she said as how she said it. What I heard was, "Oh, you poor thing, it's so cute that you think you might have a chance."

After we hung up, I felt silly, stupid. *What was I thinking? Of course, I'm not going to make it. Maybe I am just in denial.* All day long, I couldn't shake that feeling of hopelessness. *Why am I even writing that dumb book. I should just delete the whole thing. Nobody's going to want to read it anyway.*

That feeling brought back memories I hadn't thought about in a long time.

Welcome to Court Reporting

New York City 1994: As a freshly minted court reporter, I was still sleeping on my boyfriend's sister's couch but there was a light at the end of the tunnel. I was starting to pick up more steady work and that would soon provide the income I needed to secure my own apartment.

Working as a freelance court reporter meant I didn't work in a courthouse, I worked for attorneys doing depositions.

Depositions are an opportunity for attorneys to ask questions of the opposing side before a trial. It's a fact-finding endeavor to find out what the other side knows. My job is to take down a verbatim record of the questions and answers and whatever else is said while on the record and then produce a transcript. The transcript can also be used to impeach a witness's testimony if they say something different at trial versus what they said in the deposition. Sometimes the person being deposed is a plaintiff, sometimes a defendant, and sometimes it's a witness to the event or events. It can also be experts who have been retained to explain why one side is right and one side is wrong. Since I'm a freelance reporter and we are required to be impartial, I work through court reporting agencies to get my work. Attorneys hire the agency, and the agency hires me.

Invariably, when people find out what I do, they ask the question, "Aren't you afraid of technology making your job obsolete?" At which point I relay the story of my first day of court reporting school back in the fall of 1991. The couple that I nannied for had offered to pay for my schooling if I agreed to go to school at nights, allowing me to watch the children during the day.

The class started with about 30 adults ranging in ages from 19 to 50 years old, all women except for one gentleman. We all had our starter steno machines in front of us and the required theory book we purchased when we signed up for the course. The steno machine is somewhat like a typewriter except it doesn't contain all the letters of the alphabet. And unlike a typewriter, where you type one letter at a time, on a steno machine, you press multiple keys at a time. It's basically a shorthand system that allows you to write complete words and phrases with one stroke.

My first teacher was a very kind retired gentleman named Jerry Pellis, a distinguished retired court reporter who had spent over 50 years sitting in front of one of these machines. Once the class started, he began by telling us that the dropout rate for court reporting students was 95 percent. He explained the reason for that was due to several factors. One, it required an extraordinary amount of dedication and practice to achieve the requirements of obtaining a court reporting certificate.

And along with dedication, it also took a certain amount of natural ability. He compared it to playing an instrument. To be a good musician, you have to be able to read the music and play the notes without thinking about it. In court reporting, you are using your ears and not your eyes for your input. They both require your brain to take in the information, process it, and send it to your fingers in split seconds, without hesitation. Not every person is born with this skill. In the end, the majority of the class would realize it's either too much work or they wouldn't be able to attain the speeds necessary to complete the course, regardless of how much they practiced.

Already, everyone was shifting in their seats, each of us wondering, will I be one of the few to make it? I had grown up playing the saxophone and the piano, and in high school I competed in Nationals for speed typing, so I felt confident I was in the right place.

However, the next part of his introduction to court reporting had me wondering why I was there. He proceeded to read us a newspaper article outlining how new recording devices were going to soon make the court reporting profession obsolete. It explained how new technology was going to revolutionize the way courts and legal proceedings would be recorded. When he finished reading, he set the article on his desk. We all just sat there a little dumbfounded. What the heck were we doing there?

Then he explained, "That article was written in 1945. They have been trying that long to replace us and it's not going to happen."

And today they are still trying and they still haven't.

Recording devices, no matter how sophisticated, won't ask someone to repeat something if a cough or sneeze renders a statement inaudible. It also won't tell you if someone's microphone is turned off or if someone forgot to turn the recording device on. And anybody who has used the voice to text functionality on their computer or phone knows how imprecise that is. Don't get me started on people that speak with accents or mumble or constantly interrupt other speakers. I once took the testimony of a Russian chemist who kept saying what sounded like ha-ZUL-dus. At a break I asked the scientist to spell the word for me. He spelled hazardous. I wonder what the voice to text would have come up with for that.

Court reporters are certified at 225 words per minute but often are pushed to write faster than that, with 95 percent accuracy. We can also read back any question or answer within a few seconds. Sadly, the only reason we may disappear is because we have so few new people joining the profession. As the older generation of reporters begin to retire, there is not enough new blood to fill the demand.

Over My Head

Starting out in any profession can be challenging, and court reporting is no different. You have to be willing to take what other established reporters don't want. I guess you call it paying your dues. Right away when I graduated school, I sent my resume out to numerous agencies, and I also began calling them so that I could get my name out there. One agency had responded and sent me out on two jobs, which had gone fine, in fact not even memorable.

The third job of my career was the one that I will never forget.

The owner of the agency, Toby, called me directly to tell me about the job. It was an expert, a neurosurgeon, in a medical malpractice case. Just as those words penetrated my ears, my stomach gurgled. "I've never done a doctor before." I tried to warn her. I thought to myself, *not to mention, I always did poorly with medical terminology in school.*

"You'll be fine. You can do this. These don't usually go that long."

I guess if she thinks I can do it. Plus, I really need the money.

She gave me the time and address and name of the case.

The next morning, I rose early because I wanted to make sure I got there in plenty of time to set up and mentally prepare myself. My stomach was in knots as I showered and got dressed. *What happens if I can't do it? No, stop thinking that. You can do it. She wouldn't send you if she didn't think you could do it.*

I finished getting ready, picked up my soft suitcase that carried my steno machine, and headed for the train station. I was getting more and more uneasy the closer I got to Manhattan. *Why did I agree to do this? I should not have taken this assignment.* But it was too late, I no longer had a choice.

I arrived at the doctor's office in plenty of time to leisurely set up and become acquainted with my surroundings, hoping I would settle in and get more comfortable with the situation, but that's not what happened. I checked in with the receptionist and she asked me to take a seat in the waiting room. I glanced at the clock, an hour early. Perfect. I would be able to pick my spot to set up where I would be at optimal ability to hear the doctor clearly. *I got this.*

Minutes passed by as I waited for the receptionist to take me back to a conference room. 15 minutes passed and my stomach began to feel queasy again. Next thing I knew, it was

35 minutes before the deposition start time. *That's okay, still plenty of time. No big deal.*

With every minute that passed, my blood pressure increased. *Come on. Just bring me back there already.* Then it was 15 minutes prior to the start time. *It's okay. No big deal. I will just have to be assertive and tell them where I'm sitting. I will take control of this deposition, just like they taught us in school. And if I need to stop them, I will stop them. I can do this.*

Finally, with 5 minutes to go before the deposition start time, I was escorted not to a conference room, but to the doctor's medical office. It was a large room, cold and gray, with little furnishings. Placed in front of the window was a large wooden desk and two folding chairs placed in front of it. There was no table. *Where the heck am I going to set up?* Typically, in a deposition, we are in a conference room with a rectangular conference room table. I would normally sit at the head of the table with the questioning attorney on one side of me and the witness on the other side of me. That way I was assured of hearing every syllable that came out of their mouths, because that's what I am there to capture: Every. Syllable.

We are trained to focus on the words we hear and let our fingers do the rest, without even thinking about what we are writing. It's an amazing and complex relationship between our brain and our fingers. But when we hear a word we don't know or we can't hear or don't understand, it causes us to pause, actually *think*, and then it's just a snowball effect, we're so caught up in trying to figure out that one word, we've just missed the next five words that they spoke. The ability to hear clearly is critical.

Right away as I entered the room, my eyes darted around looking for an outlet to plug my machine in. I found one, just one, and it was about 10 feet from the doctor's desk. Had I been an experienced reporter, I would have had an extension cord in my bag, but I wasn't and so I didn't. It also didn't occur to me that I could ask the doctor's office for one. I said nothing. It also hadn't occurred to me to bring any sort of tape recorder as a backup. At that time, that was considered taboo. The recording device was ME.

Shortly after I set up my machine, two attorneys dressed in dark suits entered the room and introduced themselves and gave me their business cards. They were neither friendly nor rude. They explained they were from out of town and had just flown in that morning for the deposition and would be flying back home that afternoon. They also informed me that they would not be the ones doing the questioning, that there would be five attorneys on the telephone and one of them would be doing the questioning. The room felt like it was closing in on me. *Five attorneys on the telephone? This is way out of my league. Why did I agree to take this job?!*

Oh, my gosh, I can't do this. I don't know how to do this. What is going to happen if I can't do it? I can't do it. I know I can't do it. Oh, my gosh, what do I do?

Just as I was getting ready to hyperventilate, the doctor entered the room and took his place behind his desk. He was an older, heavyset man with a scowl and a balding head. He clearly was not thrilled that he was having to take the time to do this. It also appeared to be the case that his prestigious title excused him from performing niceties. He was important and he had patients to see and he wanted to get this over with. The attorneys on the phone were ready to go. I asked the doctor to raise his right hand and I swore him in and placed my trembling fingers on the keys of my steno machine.

"Doctor, can you please state your name for the record." *Okay, so far so good, I got that.*

I was able to hold on for the first 5 to 10 minutes while they went over the routine questions of where the doctor worked, his education, and his current profession. Then it all went downhill. The questions got faster and the words got harder.

"Doctor, on what date did the plaintiff undergo the intra-arterial catheterization angiography"—*The what? I have to stop them. I have no idea what he just said.*

I said, "Excuse me. Excuse me. I didn't catch that word."

All eyes in the room darted to me and looked at me like it was the first time they realized I was there. I felt my face burn up. Their annoyance was easy to detect. Meanwhile, the attorney on the phone couldn't hear me because he was still in the middle of his ridiculously long question.

The attorneys in the room and the doctor all began trying to get the attention of the attorney on the phone, "Stop. Stop. The court reporter didn't get what you said."

Finally, the attorney ended the question. The annoyed doctor said, "The court reporter didn't get the question. You'll have to repeat it."

"What did you get?" the attorney asked me. I read what I had written and he clarified the word for me.

This is going to take forever if I stop them every time. I have to do better. Come on, Kathy, pull it together. Just write what you hear and you can figure it out later.

The deposition continued and the attorney slowed down for a few questions but within just a minute or two he resumed his previous speed. Then he asked the doctor to refer to the medical record and read from it.

Why is he reading so fast? Oh, my gosh, I am not getting this. He's talking and I have no idea what he's saying.

And that was pretty much the way the next 45 minutes went. I would catch the beginning of the question, miss a few words in the middle, think to myself, *shoot, remember what he said there,* and maybe catch the end of the question. The answers were a mess. The doctor spoke fast and mumbled, and I was too far away to be able to catch all of what he was saying. Also, since I had never done a medical job before, I had no idea at that time that it was entirely appropriate for me to ask for any records that were read from.

I have never been so relieved to hear three little words, "No further questions." However, it was not savored for long. Before I could even pack up my machine, the attorneys in the room approached me and said that they would like to expedite the transcript. The usual turnaround for a transcript is 10 business days but they were wanting it in two days.

Inside I felt ill. I confidently said, "Sure," as I almost threw up in my mouth. I was hoping that they didn't notice my hands shaking as I placed my machine back in its case.

At that time, I was still working for the agency in Manhattan doing office work until I had more steady court reporting work, and they were nice enough to allow me to work on my transcripts there since I didn't have my own computer yet. My goal was to someday take court reporting jobs for this agency, but all of their work was very technical and not appropriate for new reporters.

When I got to the office, I immediately inserted the disk from my steno machine into the computer and translated my notes from steno into English. The way the software works is you create a personal dictionary that tells the computer that every time you stroke these certain keys, it means this word in English. Obviously the bigger the dictionary, the more words that are turned from steno into English. Words that are not in your dictionary are called untranslates. They appear in the transcript as capital letters called steno and are typically highlighted or in different colored font so that they are easily recognizable.

I was really hoping that if I started working on the transcript while it was fresh in my head, that I could hopefully piece it together enough to have a resemblance of what was said. However, as I opened up the transcript and began to read, I felt the nausea returning, growing more severe with the more I read. I went through it quickly at first and fixed all the obvious corrections. That still left gaping holes where I am sure some medical terms were said. After spending hours trying to figure out what some of the words could be, trying to remember what I told myself to remember, I realized that I was in way over my head. I was going to have to come clean to the agency. I made the dreaded call.

"Hi Toby, it's Kathy."

"Hi, Kathy. How did it go?"

"Well, not that good."

"What happened?"

I explained the whole scenario with having to set up too far away, the attorneys on the phone, the doctor reading too fast and mumbling. Surprisingly, Toby was very understanding at first. She asked me to send her the transcript and she would have a nurse friend take a look at it. "I'm sure it's fine," she assured me.

What a relief I felt! Still somewhat doubtful and completely embarrassed to be in this situation, I was glad to have the help. However, after they looked at it, they decided they couldn't do anything with it either, and I got a call from Toby.

"Kathy, that transcript is a mess. We couldn't decipher most of it. I don't know what we're going to do. We might have to pay for a whole new deposition, that means paying for the attorneys and the doctor. This could cost us thousands of dollars."

I felt tears forming in my eyes and my stomach turned. I could barely squeak out a "sorry."

She continued, "I'm sorry, but I think you should reconsider being a court reporter. I don't think you have what it takes to do this job."

That destroyed me. Tears started pouring out of my eyes in complete defeat. *I can't reconsider! This is all I have! I've worked so hard to get here and I HAVE to do this. I can't support myself without this job and I have no backup.* I had been counting on this career and I saw this as my only way out. I couldn't continue to live on Sharon's couch, and without this job, I couldn't afford to live on my own. I felt like my whole world just crumbled. I was a gigantic failure.

Needless to say, I never worked for her again. I would come to find out that Toby had been a reporter for 30 years and refused to do medical jobs. Looking back at that job now, it was like sending a brand-new driver to the Indy 500 in Daytona to race. It was positively ludicrous for her to send me on that job. Thankfully the case settled and so the attorneys were willing to let it go without being transcribed.

I don't know how, but somehow I found the courage to keep going. If I'm being honest, it was out of necessity more than it was courage. I just didn't see any other choices. Plus, in my heart, I knew I could do this job. And I was right. 30 years later and I'm still enjoying the challenge and complexities of this career. I have climbed to the top of my profession because I refused to listen to what one person told me I couldn't do. And I won't start listening to them now.

CHAPTER 10

Figure It Out

I look out the window a lot these days. The weather is warming up. The trees have flowered and brought forth their summer leaves. Birds are singing their sweet songs. I remember back when I was diagnosed that I didn't think I would see another spring, yet here I am, 10 months later, taking each day as a gift.

We have a patio just outside where I sit in the living room and so I can feel the warm spring breeze waft into the apartment from the open door that leads to it. When I see people pass by on their way to the park, often with young children or pets, or both, I watch them walking and try to remember what that felt like, to walk without any thought. I want to tell them, don't take it for granted, enjoy every minute. But where does that desire come from, to admonish people to take more delight in something we no longer possess? Do we think that if we had just appreciated something more at the time we had it, that we wouldn't be missing it now that it's gone? I can prove that theory wrong because I remember always being very grateful for my ability to walk, especially when I would see someone in a wheelchair, and guess what, I don't miss it any less now that my ability to walk is getting closer and closer to being nonexistent.

"Figure it out." I feel like somewhere amidst one of my periods of upheaval and uncertainty someone told me to just "figure it out" and it has become sort of a mantra for me. Especially lately. As I head into the eleventh month of my diagnosis, my body continues to rebel against my wishes. My feet have become a couple of teenagers. I tell them to move over just an inch or two, and they pretend not to hear me. I feel like they have teamed up to see how frustrated they can make me. Most days I don't let them get to me, but every now and then I give them a solid curse under my breath.

A large portion of my days now consists of figuring it out. Figuring out how to stand up, how to sit down, how to put on my socks. Forget shoes, I've had to let that luxury go as my feet have become more swollen. Just as I make peace with where I am at with my symptoms and abilities (or lack thereof), everything gets a little harder; my arms become more tingly, my hands become more numb, and my legs become weaker. The tasks I have had to figure out and adjust to, I have to figure out all over again.

At the same time, I have stopped telling people, and myself, that it can't get much harder and that I probably won't be able to walk soon, because I realized that I have been repeating that statement for the last 6 months, and here I am, still walking. My pace has steadily decreased but my legs are still getting the job done. That's all I can ask for at this point.

The other morning, I was lying in bed and contemplating my relationship with my body. When I was an adolescent, I had the typical self-consciousness that most teenage girls feel. I wasn't overweight but as my mother liked to say, I was "big-boned." By the time I was 13 years old, I had reached my mature height of 5'6-1/2" which meant that I towered over most of the girls and practically all of the boys in my class. However, as I got older, I came to appreciate my body more, especially as I got into my 20s. I always had strong legs and I was happy with how they looked.

When I reached my 30s and 40s, my appreciation grew not so much in how my body looked but of how healthy my body had always been. After hearing of other people's ailments with their bodies, I realized how lucky I was to have the body that God had given me. Other than a couple of bunions that I inherited from my grandmother and my mother, which, if I wore the right shoes, didn't bother me at all, I had lived my first 45 years without any major health problems. I hadn't broken a bone, spent a night in the hospital, or even been stung by a bee.

The closer I got to God, the more I began to see my body as a mere vessel, like a car. I appreciated the reliability of it. I believed that if I took care of it, did the routine maintenance, that it would last me many years. I often spoke words of gratitude for my body during my daily prayers or sometimes in my hot yoga classes, when I was feeling strong and much younger than my age would suggest I should feel.

When I was 40 years old, I also developed an interest in doing all that I could to maintain the health of my body. I started eating mostly vegan. I did a sweep of all of our household cleaning products and personal hygiene products and discarded anything with known toxins and replaced them with more natural options. I attended hot yoga at least two to four days a week. I did everything I could to treat my body like I would a Lamborghini or Maserati. Even as my body aged, I could look in the mirror and be content with what reflected back.

At 50 years old I was definitely showing my fair share of wrinkles and cellulite, but that didn't bother me much because I always believed that what was under the hood was what mattered, and I had a fine-tuned engine inside of me. I was okay with a little bit of wear and tear on the outside as long as the internal components still hummed like a bee. And then my check engine light came on.

Cancer Diagnosis

When I first felt the lump in my left breast at the end of 2019, I tried to ignore it. How could there be anything wrong? I felt fine. Months went by and the light was still on, the lump getting larger. When it was finally diagnosed it was Stage 2 IDC, invasive ductal carcinoma. From what the doctors could tell, it had not spread to the lymph nodes. My next step after being diagnosed was not to meet with an oncologist but to meet with a surgeon. She recommended a full mastectomy (because the lump was too large for a lumpectomy), she wanted to put me into early menopause, and she wanted to put me on Tamoxifen for the rest of my life.

After all the reading I had done about health, that didn't sit right with me. Both Chris and I felt that it was too extreme. Not to mention, Tamoxifen is known to cause ovarian cancer. That's when I was introduced to a book called "Chris Beat Cancer" by Chris Wark who was diagnosed with stage 4 colon cancer at the age of 26. After undergoing emergency surgery, he refused to do the chemotherapy that the doctors were insisting was necessary. They told him he was *insane* if he didn't. But Chris Wark held onto his instinct and refused to do chemo, opting instead to research other nontoxic treatments. He started with his diet, eating mostly raw fruits and vegetables for 3 months and then transitioning to a plant-based diet. He began juicing, exercising, meditating, praying. The survival rate for his type of cancer at his age was roughly 25 percent. Now, almost 20 years later, still cancer-free, he is an advocate of treating cancer holistically.

Along with starting Chris Wark's program, I did other reading and started to integrate other regimens into my new life. One was the Gerson therapy which consisted of juicing 4 pounds of apples and 4 pounds of carrots every day. Every morning Chris would get up at 5 am and juice for me. Let me just interject and state that there is nothing sexier than a man in his T-shirt and boxer shorts with bed-head juicing apples and carrots for you.

Another part of the Gerson therapy was coffee enemas. I was a little hesitant to start those, just because, I mean, it's a coffee enema. I loved coffee but I preferred drinking it as opposed to, well, you know. But four months into my diagnosis, I was getting a massage and my chatty massage therapist was telling me how another client of hers swore that she got rid of her cancer by coffee enemas. That was all I needed to hear. Coffee enemas it was. Gerson therapy recommended four to five enemas a day but that was too time consuming. I was still working and that just didn't seem conceivable. I started with one a day, and once I got the hang of it, I began doing two a day. I did two coffee enemas a day for six months and my lump was gone. Completely gone. And it's still gone.

However, six months after that, in July of 2021, I began to feel a small lump under my left armpit. I did a full body scan with thermography and nothing threatening showed up. Throughout the next few months, I met with a naturopath who was certified in internal medicine, and we tried different supplements and treatments but the lymph node continued to grow.

Now, I'm sure many people will say that I was foolish for not opting for the mastectomy and following the surgeon's recommendation. And maybe they're right. We'll never know, of course. But I believe in my gut that I did the right thing for me. And I truly sense that even if I had pursued conventional treatments, I suspect I would still find myself in the same battle today.

One thing I won't ever do is criticize other's choices in treating their cancer, recognizing that it is a deeply personal decision. Individuals must determine what works best for them. Whichever method they select, conventional or holistic, is a leap of faith. There are no guarantees with either. For myself, it was important that I remove the fear component and follow my own gut instinct and my own research. Once I made my decision, I vowed to myself that I would have no regrets, regardless of the outcome.

Today, my relationship with my body is a little different. I try not to be disappointed with it. In all honesty, I'm still pretty impressed by it. Every part of me is working so hard. It has become a team effort between my brain and my limbs. However, sadly, I am forgetting what it felt like to be normal, strong. My legs feel like I am wearing soaking wet jeans, the tightness and heaviness. My arms, back, and neck feel like I am wearing a wet shirt. I am starting to feel more sensations in my head. My whole body is now affected by this monster in my spine. The list of tasks that I am able to do keeps getting shorter, yet I remind myself constantly how lucky I am. Almost a year into this diagnosis and I still have control of my bowel and bladder. That itself is perhaps a miracle.

I was watching a movie last night and there was a scene with a large gala and people dancing. Tears came to my eyes. I have always wanted to take dancing lessons. For years, I have said that I was going to do it. And my husband has always agreed that it would be a fun thing to do, yet we never made the time to do it. Why? Why do we just assume that we will have unlimited time to do all the things that we want to do? We have all heard the admonition before, don't put off enjoying life, don't take life for granted, yet we all do it.

I still focus on the present day, but it becomes more and more challenging not to think of what happens next, when

– I mean IF – I am no longer able to walk. I am constantly reminding myself that I do not know the future. Things could turn around any day now. On the one hand, I am desperate to flip to the end of the book and see how this story ends. But on the other hand, I know there is a reason we are not privy to such information. For example, if I knew that I wasn't going to make it, would I just give up, thinking what's the point? But in doing so, I may miss out on one last adventure, one last interaction with a friend, one last date night with my husband.

Every time I tell myself that I can't take much more, my time has to be getting close, I think of Maddie. Maddie is my best friend Dawn's little Coton de Tulear, a little fluffy dog with a huge personality. This pint size bundle of energy is quite a little survivor. As a puppy she had been hit by a car and spent several nights in the veterinary hospital, requiring surgery to correct her broken leg. A slight limp was all that resulted from it. Then a few years ago she contracted some random virus that wreaked havoc on her kidneys. Dawn was told that she would likely go into kidney failure, but to the amazement of everyone at the vet's office, she pulled through again. Damage had been done to the kidneys and so she required medication, but other than that, she was going to be okay. But that's not why I think of her.

Back in February, Chris informed me that he had qualified for an all-expense paid trip to Nashville by his company for being one of the top performers. We both knew that it wasn't feasible for me to accompany him, but we also realized that I couldn't stay by myself. I really wanted Chris to go on this trip because I wanted him to have a break from me. Not that he ever complained, but I knew it would be good for him. Shoot, I wanted a break from me. So the only question was, who can we ask to stay with me?

The first person who came to mind was Dawn. I hadn't seen her since the previous summer, although we talked almost every week via FaceTime. However, I wrestled with the idea of asking Dawn because she had, in the last few years, left her very lucrative job in corporate America to follow where God would lead her. It had been a long process of prayer and inner searching and she found herself exactly where she was meant to be, doing massage therapy and also doing spiritual direction. Needless to say, however, the pay is not exactly in line with what she had been accustomed to and so she has learned to live a lifestyle more commensurate with her income.

I knew that asking her to come stay with me for five days could be a huge financial burden for her, but I couldn't shake the feeling that I needed to at least ask and give her the opportunity to say no. Also, the more I prayed about it, the more I felt like I needed to invite Glenda. I knew that Glenda had a very busy job in a mental health facility, and I had no idea if she could take the time off, yet I couldn't shake the feeling that Glenda had to be included in the invite. I finally decided that I would just ask them both and then if they both said no, which is what I expected, well, at least I asked.

When I was chatting with Dawn on our weekly call, I told her, "Dawn, I have something to ask but I want you to know it's totally okay for you to say no. In fact, you don't even have to answer right now."

Before I could continue, Dawn jumped in, "Okay, but then I have something to ask you."

"Okay. Chris is going out of town in April and I was wondering if you and Glenda would want to come stay with me." And then I quickly said, before she could even reply, "But I know that's asking a lot from you and so I am totally okay if you say no."

Dawn burst into tears. "Kathy, Glenda came to me two days ago and said I really want to go see Kath. We've been looking at dates to come see you."

Then we were both pushing tears off of our cheeks. God just never ceases to amaze me.

About two weeks before their visit, Dawn told me that Madds had started to take a turn for the worse. Her little kidneys had taken about all they could take and she now required a dialysis of sorts. It was an injection of fluid that she would need daily. The process was not an easy one to administer and she had recruited the help of others to perform the task. The concern, however, was what to do with her while Dawn was gone. With her specific needs, there was no one she could ask to keep her. Dawn had mentioned to me that she might have to bring her with to St. Louis. In my mind, I cringed. Our dog Stephi was a big dog and quite hostile towards little dogs. But I couldn't tell Dawn that she couldn't bring her. I knew I just had to pray about it. And if Dawn needed to bring Maddie, then it would be okay. Stephi would somehow be okay with her.

The trip got closer and closer. Still no options were being presented to Dawn for Maddie. I continued to pray, *God, I trust you. I know this trip was all your idea and so I know you will take care of this. Whatever happens, it will all work out. I trust you completely.*

Days before the trip, Dawn called the vet's office to see if they had any ideas. Her vet, a very kind, compassionate man, looked at his schedule to see if he could take her, but he would be out of town. He said he would speak to the staff and see if anyone was available. "What is the plan if we can't find somebody?" he asked.

Dawn had replied, "I guess I'll bring her with me to St. Louis."

"You'll be driving?"

"No, flying."

"Oh."

Dawn said there was no mistaking his tone. That obviously concerned him.

"She can't fly. It would be very detrimental to her health. In fact, I'm not sure she would survive the flight."

Dawn's heart sank.

"Let me see what we can do and I'll call you back."

The day before the trip, the vet's office called and one of the vet technicians had volunteered to come to Dawn's house every day to administer the medication, driving an hour each way to do so. On top of that, Dawn's next-door neighbors, a family she had become very close to over the years, also offered to help and bring Maddie over to their place during the day.

In the end, not only was Maddie being taken care of, but she had the best medical care and she was being watched by people that she had known and loved her whole life. We couldn't have planned it better ourselves. And even though it had come down to the wire and we were all concerned that they wouldn't be able to come, God knew all along and stepped in just in time. And so every time I start to worry about my future, I remember Maddie. God took care of every detail in ways that weren't even fathomable to us. And if God would do all of that for Maddie, of course He will do the same for me. I just need to be patient and keep praying, *God, you're good and I trust you completely.* And in God's time, everything is going to work out perfectly.

CHAPTER 11

Trust Through The Tears

In just one month, it will mark the one-year anniversary of my diagnosis. My world continues to get smaller and smaller. The kitchen is now a daunting voyage for me. I may have the stamina to get there, but I have to contemplate if I will have the fortitude to return. It's been days since I've felt up to the task, lacking the confidence that I can make it both ways.

I'm spending more time in bed these days because it's easier for me to stand up from the bed than it is our living room sofa. Since our sofa sits lower, I have to rely on my arm strength to lift my body to a standing position. I've discovered that I only have one or two of those lifts in me per day and so I choose to ration them for the evening so I can sit with Chris, and we can eat dinner together and watch some television before bed. It's nice sitting next to him on the couch. It feels normal and normal feels amazing.

What I miss the most about my prior life is feeling close to my husband. I'm no longer able to stand and hug him or cuddle up behind him in bed while he's sleeping. I have become an island. At least while I am sitting next to him, we can enjoy some normalcy. We will hold hands. Most nights he will rub my neck. I will scratch his back. I feel so indebted to him for all that he does for me but he insists that he is doing what a husband is supposed to do because he loves me. His sweet kisses every morning remind me how blessed I am that God chose him for me, and that once we get through this chapter in our lives and I am restored, our marriage will be stronger than ever.

I'm also trying to stay grateful for all that I can still do. And when I have to delete something from the list, I try not to dwell on it.

However, I still have days of feeling defeated, worn out. Those are the loneliest days. *Maybe I'm foolish for thinking I have any hope. Maybe I'm just another person with cancer who will die way too young. Maybe God doesn't love me like I thought He did.* And I hate those thoughts. It makes me feel entitled and spoiled, like a victim.

For a while, I started to cut myself off from people. I figured, if I'm tired of myself, everybody else should be tired of me too. I just wanted to get through the days as quickly as possible so that I could X out another day on the calendar, knowing that that made me one day closer to....to what? I don't even know. I guess the end, whatever that is. And at this point I don't even care.

Death, too, began to occupy my thoughts - not so much what comes after you die, I feel pretty confident in that arena, but rather my own impending demise. It's the old adage, "I'm not afraid of dying, I just don't want to be there when it happens." And I don't wonder about death in general, I wonder about *my* death. IF that is God's will for me, will I be in pain? Will it be scary? I often pray and I tell God, *I really do not want my last breaths on earth to be terrifying. Please let me just slip away peacefully. Jesus, let me fall asleep in Chris's arms and wake up in yours.* And, really, that's true for whenever I die, even if it's not for another 50 years. However, at this time it feels as though it may happen sooner rather than later.

And then I'm reminded of the scene from the movie Beaches where Barbara Hersey's character, Hillary, who has a terminal illness, is at her beach house with her best friend, Bette Midler's character, CC. Hillary starts withdrawing from other friends, her daughter, her life. She becomes sullen and angry. When CC confronts her, Hillary accuses CC of not understanding. After all, she was still in the land of the living. CC, being the amazing friend she is, reminds Hillary, "Well, so are you. You're not dead yet."

And that's what I am trying to remember. Since I'm still here, God is obviously not done with me. There is still purpose for me here. *God, once again I thank you for all of this, even though I don't like it. Please fill me with your peace and show me what I can do to fulfill your plan for me.*

CHAPTER 12

Let The Cross Transform You

Weeks away from the one-year anniversary of my diagnosis, my biggest fear became reality. As I was attempting to walk with my walker into the bedroom, my legs finally turned in their resignation, effective immediately, causing me to crumple and somehow break my ankle. As a result, I am now relegated to my bed or wheelchair and I am completely dependent on my husband to bring me food, bring me to the shower, to the toilet, help me dress. I've been telling myself that if I ever got where I couldn't walk, that that would be it for me. I would want to quit, give up, decide that life was not worth living.

I won't lie, I had a few days feeling like that. And then something wonderful happened. God's grace. His beautiful grace. He has once again filled me with awe and gratitude for this whole experience.

Today I was sitting on our little patio, enjoying my morning coffee and the view that was before me. Chris loves plants and herbs and watching things grow and he has turned our little corner patio into a mini botanical garden. On our patio we have pots and pots of different herbs and ferns and plants. Extending beyond our patio, technically in the domain of the apartment complex, he has planted many other plants, one of which is elephant ears, my favorite. I can't help but marvel at how quickly they grow, each one sprouting off the back of a prior one. Along with the plants and a birdbath, he has hung two bird feeders, a flowering hanging plant, and a melodious windchime, creating a sanctuary of tranquility.

Today, the backdrop to all of this beauty is a light gray sky producing fine and steady rain. The sound is soothing, calming. The rain has painted all of the tree trunks and branches a brilliant black and transformed the leaves into a vibrant green. I am engulfed in sublimity.

God, I thank you for granting me eyes to behold the wonders you have created.

I find myself saddened for anybody who is blind and not able to take in such beauty. What a horrible way to go through life, I imagine.

Blindness sounds dreadful to me because that's not my cross.

"It's not your cross to bear" used to confuse me when I was younger. What exactly did that mean? What it means to me now is that everybody has something they struggle with, that weighs them down. It could be addiction, anxiety, an abusive spouse, dysfunctional family, or an illness. It's the thing that brings you to your knees, causing you to have pain, to suffer, to cry out and question God's love for you. And you can either let that cross destroy you or transform you. Fear and faith cannot reside together because they both want the same thing from you: Fear wants you to believe something that hasn't happened yet. And faith wants you to believe something that hasn't happened yet. Which will you choose?

I heard once that if people were allowed to toss their ailment (or struggle) into a giant hat mixed with everybody else's, and then were given the choice to pick a new unknown ailment or have their own ailment back, that most people would want to pick their own. I know for me, each time I've thought of that, regardless of what I was going through, even now, I would pick my own. The old Irish proverb rings true, "Better the devil you know." However awful your current situation, the unknown is even more daunting.

I think it is human nature to say, "If [blank] happened to me, I couldn't handle it."

God wants me to tell you that whatever cross it is that you have to bear, He wants to help you through it. He wants to use this to transform you into a new life, a better life. And it may seem impossible, and you may not be able to see how that could possibly happen, but God does. Because with God, there are no limits to what He can do.

Chaga me!

In January of 2022, before my current diagnosis, my friend Lorna from Minnesota texted me about a woman she knew named Katy. Katy had recently been diagnosed with stage 4 ovarian cancer. She had undergone multiple surgeries in an attempt to eradicate all the cancer, but the long-term survival rate for this type of cancer was bleak. Lorna had mentioned to Katy all the things I did to get rid of my cancer, and Katy was curious about what I had done. Lorna passed on my number to Katy, and Katy and I struck up an immediate friendship. Despite all that she was going through, she displayed a sense of humor and friendliness that I was easily drawn to.

I learned that Katy was in her mid-40s, married, with three kids ranging from elementary school to high school. As we chatted and got to know one another, we sent pictures so we had a visual of each other. She sent me a picture of her and her best buds taken just days before her diagnosis. It was a warm sunny day in the summer and she and her friends were enjoying an outdoor concert. When you look at this woman smiling at the camera, her petite athletic build, blond hair and tan skin, she's the last person you would suspect of possessing inside her a gruesome cancer that wants to destroy her. She is now living every woman's worst nightmare. She has undergone multiple surgeries and numerous rounds of chemotherapy and continues to fight so that she may hopefully beat the odds and be there to watch her children grow, celebrate all of their big life moments with them, and grow old with her husband.

We chatted intermittently on and off for the next 6 months, encouraging each other through all the ups and downs that accompany a cancer diagnosis. Even when tests are coming back with favorable results, every twinge of pain or discomfort is presumed to be the cancer wreaking havoc on you, allowing your underlying fear to push its ugly head to the front of the crowd, until you fart or burp and realize it was just gas. The roller coaster is never ending, and Katy and I were seated in the first car, holding hands, and riding every twist and turn together.

When I was diagnosed in June, I held off reaching out to her. I hated to tell her the news. She was already filled with angst about her situation, and I didn't want to add to her burden. However, within a few weeks, as was typical if too much time had passed, she reached out to me and I shared my news with her. In true friend form, she was shocked and devastated and pissed off.

The next couple of months passed with slightly more frequent texts of care and support on both ends. Then, one Sunday evening in August, Chris and I were enjoying dinner with his boys. I noticed a text from Katy come across my phone just as we were getting ready to eat. I glanced at it but I ignored it until dinner was over, dessert was enjoyed, and the boys headed home.

As I made myself comfortable on the couch to recuperate from a busy day, I opened Katy's text, and as I read it, my heart started pounding:

> *"Kathy!! I literally cannot type this message fast enough. You have been on my mind constantly since you shared your recent setback. I was visibly upset this morning when a friend of mine asked what was weighing so heavy on me. I shared that my heart was broken for you. We prayed together for you and unbeknownst to me she reached out to another mutual friend of ours and shared your story. This woman happens to sit on the board of a company that is doing promising new cancer research. She hadn't brought it up to me prior to this because I'm not a candidate for their trial. Currently they are only taking patients where conventional therapy is no longer an option. She explained it to me and it sounds amazing and the results they have seen so far (it's early pre clinical data and only a handful of patients) but all have seen tumor regression. ALL!! It's derived from mushrooms. Go figure. The clinical liaison is waiting for your call and can explain everything. They are holding a spot for you in the trial if you want it. I'm covered in goosebumps!"*

I read the text over again. She had also attached the contact information for the liaison, Alyssa. I read the text to my husband. Neither of us knew what to make of this. *God is God and He can do anything* floated around in my head. *Is this you, God? It sounds too good to be true but I also know that's how you roll.*

For a second, I thought about waiting until the following day, Monday, to make the call, but I knew I wouldn't be able to sleep if I waited. *I'll feel better even if I have to leave a message.*

And that's what I did. However, within 10 minutes, Alyssa's name was showing up on my phone as an incoming call and my heart jumped again.

In the next 30 minutes I would learn that Alyssa is actually the one that developed the mushroom concoction. She lives in Minnesota just south of Minneapolis and she has a farm with horses. One of her beloved horses, Poppy, developed cancer, and the tumors were near his throat. As the tumors grew in size, it was making it difficult for him to breathe.

Alyssa, with her biochem and pharmaceutical degrees, attempted to find a way to shrink the tumors just enough so that Poppy could breathe better. It came as quite a surprise to her that the formula she developed not only shrunk the cancer, but it also eradicated it completely. In fact, it reversed it to the point that there were zero cancer cells remaining.

Realizing that what she had done had been nothing short of miraculous, she knew she had to figure out a way to make it consumable for humans. After all, she had promised God that that's what she would do.

When Alyssa's horse became ill, she asked God to help her. And in that prayer, she made a solemn vow that if He would help her heal her faithful horse, that she would do all she could to bring it to the human population. When Poppy went into complete remission, Alyssa knew she had a new mission to develop this mushroom formula to save people. And so far, that is what she has done.

Within a few weeks I was on the mushroom protocol, a daily dose of a mushroom-based drink. I started with just a few ounces and now I am up to 36 ounces a day. It is easy to consume with a mild taste resembling a faint root beer flavor. It is not thick or chunky, it just has a slightly oily texture. I've been drinking it daily now for the past 10 months. There is no doubt in my mind that this is part of the reason I am still here today.

Recently my friends Tammy and Lorna visited me. Lorna and I reminisced about how it all started with her introduction to Katy. When Lorna first told me about Katy, it was my impression that they were somewhat friendly. Lorna corrected my interpretation.

"Kathy, I barely know Katy. I had run into her three different times in one week until I finally I told her about you. And since then, I haven't seen her at all."

Katy and I have never spoken other than via text. I have no idea what Alyssa looks like. Yet these two women have become pivotal people in my life. I feel a connection to them in a very special way, like they were very purposely and strategically placed in my life with great importance and meaning.

God, this has to be you. From Lorna, to Katy, to Katy's friend, to Katy's friend's friend, and ultimately to Alyssa and her mushroom formula. I have to wonder, why would you take me this far if it wasn't to save me? And yet I can't presume to know your plans. Thank you, God, that I don't need to do anything but trust you.

Whatever God's plan is, I know what I have to do. I have to continue on with patience and gratitude and faith in the knowledge that whatever my future holds, I don't need to fear it. God will provide the grace I need for any situation. Isn't that what He's been doing my whole life?

Divine Mercy

Along with the mushroom drink, Chris and I adopted another daily practice that has profoundly impacted our lives.

July 2023: In the initial months following my terminal diagnosis, we reverted back to the routine we established during my first battle with breast cancer. This included juicing 4 pounds of apples and 4 pounds of carrots every day.

One Monday morning stands out vividly in my memory. Both Chris and I rose early, with Chris initiating the juicing process while I tackled some work before my 9 a.m. deposition. As I attempted to submit a transcript through the agency website, frustration mounted when the portal failed to cooperate. Time was ticking and my patience waned. All of a sudden, a loud crash echoed from the kitchen, accompanied by an expletive from Chris.

"What's wrong?" I called out from the office.

"The juicer just broke!" Chris exclaimed, as he angrily began mopping up all the juice that had escaped onto the counter and began spilling over onto the floor.

Frustration permeated the apartment as I struggled with my work and Chris dealt with the aftermath of the juicer mishap. It wasn't long and I heard another stream of choice words from the kitchen.

"Now what?' I asked.

"The French press just fell apart! There's coffee all over the place!"

Lord, what is going on this morning?

Eventually, I managed to submit my transcript while Chris cleaned up the coffee fiasco. As I prepared for my deposition, Chris settled behind his desk in the office that we shared. Within a few minutes, Chris received an unexpected phone call from a number he didn't recognize. He almost ignored it, but something told him to answer it.

"Hello?"

"Is this Chris Heeb, the publisher of Clayton Parish Neighbors?" the gentleman on the other end of the line inquired.

"Yes, speaking." Chris replied.

In the preceding six months, Chris had taken on the role of publisher for the first monthly Catholic magazine in St. Louis, with a mission to reignite the faith of inactive Catholics. For years, Chris had become very frustrated with the current state of affairs within the Catholic Church. He was determined to do something about it after his father died in November 2021.

Donald Heeb had left an indelible impression at St John Vianney High School, where he was a teacher and football coach to thousands of young men over a career spanning 37 years. Coach Heeb was somewhat of a celebrity in St. Louis. In fact, the football field at Vianney is named Don Heeb Field. Upon his passing, Chris was overwhelmed with gratitude as so many former players and students showed a tremendous outpouring of love and support for his father. Chris felt his legacy was to make a difference in his faith as the cornerstone of his mission. The magazine had numerous articles based on the Catholic magisterium, along with local stories, upcoming events, and parish news in the community.

"My name is John Lally and I just wanted to let you know we received your magazine in the mail recently, I read it from cover to cover and I really enjoyed it. Thank you so much for putting out such a fine magazine. We need this in our community – a breath of fresh air!"

Instantly, Chris's mood was transformed. Chris and John began to chat, and John asked if Chris was related to Coach Don Heeb. This led to a conversation about Chris's father, Don Heeb, and his recent death. John let Chris know what a special man Coach Heeb was in the community, even though he had never met him or knew him personally.

Then John said, "Can I tell you a story about my dad?"

"Sure," Chris replied.

"My dad was diagnosed with stage 4 colon cancer, and it spread throughout his body. The doctors had told our family there was nothing they could do anymore, and that he should get his affairs in order. They told him he had just a few months to live. My mother and I began to plan his funeral."

He continued, "My dad is the former President of St. Louis Catholic Charities, and he was very good friends with St. Louis Archbishop Regali. At the time, Pope John Paul II was scheduled to arrive in St. Louis. My father asked if he could receive communion from the Pope before he died. My father was granted this request, and the now Saint John Paul II gave him the Holy Eucharist but insisted he recite daily a healing prayer called The Divine Mercy Chaplet. My father and mother began to pray this prayer every day. Chris, that was 20+ years ago and he's still alive! He's 90+ years old now! Within a few years, the cancer was gone. The reason why I tell you this story is I want you to understand the power of prayer, Chris... the power of prayer."

Chris's eyes filled with tears. "John, you have no idea what I'm going through right now with my wife."

Chris shared our situation, and it was obvious to them both that John's phone call that morning had been inspired by God. The day that started out with annoyance and exasperation was transformed into hope and faith.

The Divine Mercy Chaplet is from the diary of Saint Faustina. She was a Polish Catholic religious sister who had apparitions of Jesus which inspired the mercy chaplet. She lived from 1905 to 1938. Throughout her life she had visions and conversations with Jesus and she noted them in her diary. There are several miracles that are associated with Saint Faustina and the Chaplet of the Divine Mercy. On Divine Mercy Sunday, April 30, 2000, Pope John Paul II canonized St. Faustina Kowalska and declared the second Sunday of Easter as Divine Mercy Sunday.

Every night since that day, Chris and I have listened to the prayer on the Hallow app, which is an American Catholic meditation and prayer app, before we go to sleep. Also, on our dresser directly in front of our bed we have a first degree relic from Saint Faustina, who was Blessed Faustina at the time, given to us by Mr. and Mrs. Lally. Throughout history relics have been a source of miraculous healing, inspiration of faith, and advancement of God's Kingdom. These miracles have been documented, even beginning in the scriptures.

God, thank you for transforming our day and our lives with your grace and mercy. You never stop showing us how much you love us.

CHAPTER 13

Suffering The Kindness Of Others

There is, shall we say, a perk to being diagnosed with a terminal illness. It's a sentiment I express almost apologetically, though I'm not entirely sure why. Throughout this past year with all of its challenges, what's struck me most profoundly is the overwhelming outpouring of love from friends and family. While I always knew they cared for me, the depths of their affection and the lengths they would go to demonstrate it have been truly astonishing. Thanks to my illness, I have had the opportunity to spend time with them that I most probably wouldn't have if not for this diagnosis. We've had deep and meaningful conversations that have brought us even closer. We have shared our feelings for each other, our love, our appreciation. In a sense, I feel as if I have been allowed to attend my own funeral. How extraordinary.

"Suffering the kindness of others" is a term I heard so long ago that I can't remember the author or the circumstances, yet it resonated with me deeply and remained etched in my memory. As someone who has struggled with asking for and accepting help from others, preferring greatly to be on the other end of that relationship, my current circumstances have forced me to humble myself and be open to receiving. Once again, God's mercy has revealed the importance of allowing others to bless me. If not for people like me, in need, where would the givers go?

"It's better to give than to receive" is a wise and helpful adage to instill in our children, but let's not assume from that that receiving is less meaningful. I have learned firsthand, acts of tenderness and mercy have touched places in my heart I didn't know existed. As a result, I now long for the day when I can reach out in the same manner and help others like I have been. We all have seasons during our lives when we fall into one or the other category and God has designed us that way. These two classifications rely on each other. Without the sufferers, the underprivileged, the broken, how do givers teach future generations what compassion and kindness look like?

Three months after receiving the devastating diagnosis, I made the decision to visit my family and friends in Minnesota. Since I wasn't sure how much longer I had, I wanted one last chance to hug them and tell them in person how much each of them has meant to me. I also wanted to relax by a lake one more time. Growing up in Minnesota, the tranquility and serenity found by gazing at a calm lake at sunrise or sunset was passed down through the generations and imbedded in your genes. Ask any Minnesotan, and they will testify to the reverence that the beginning or ending sun on a lake demands. It's powerful enough that these northerners will withstand months of brutal cold and snow just to hear the melody of a Loon in the spring. Life just seems to slow down at the lake. It commands deep breaths and stillness. For many, it's their religion. It's where they find peace and closeness to their Creator.

Years ago, my sister and her husband were able to fulfill a lifetime dream of purchasing a home on the lake and nothing makes them happier than sharing their little piece of heaven with others. They share it the same way they share their faith in Jesus, openly and with a loving heart, making gratitude the cornerstone of our family gatherings.

To an outsider, it could appear as though our family had never had discord or disputes, but that would be an incorrect assumption. We have had our share of disagreements and arguments. We've hurt each other's feelings. Relationships have been severed. But in the end, we all acknowledged that family was too important to throw away. At the core, we recognized that each of us had good intentions, just different opinions. Terry, Sherry, and I finally decided that we would do a restart. The past would be put in the past. We wiped the slate clean and set some healthy boundaries. We gave each other permission to voice our opinions, and if our opinions didn't match, we agreed to disagree and move on, understanding that our differences didn't diminish our love for one another. And that has worked for us.

Today, my brother and sister and I are closer than ever. There is a grace present now that was lacking before. We still don't agree on everything, but we share faith in God and that is the glue that holds us together. As we've gotten older, we find that what we agree on far outweighs what we don't. The love I have for my siblings was rooted from a young age, and despite the storms and droughts, it has flourished into a strong and mighty connection.

Never was that connection more celebrated than that week I spent at my sister's. Terry came with his family for the long weekend. Sherry's kids and their families came. My friends came for an afternoon. The house was a constant flow of people. Laughter and conversation echoed from morning to night. The warm and sunny deck ebbed and flowed with different family members and friends and the love was palpable.

Sherry and Tom, with the help of my nephews Tanner and Taylor (who also live with them), were the perfect hosts. They prepared delicious meals for any and all who happened to be present during that time. Taylor captained pontoon rides in the afternoons. As my brother aided me in walking, he wore my arm entwined with his like a badge of honor. Relaxed games of corn hole took place on the lawn near the dock. Evenings were spent on the deck, sharing stories we had all shared a hundred times but still enjoyed.

We all knew why I was there, yet it was not a sad or melancholy atmosphere. The majority of our discussions centered on gratitude. Internally, I thought, how could I be anything but? I had been blessed with this amazing family and a life filled with deep true love and incredible adventures. I was given so much more than many others.

On the last night of my stay, after everyone else had gone to bed, the kitchen lights were dimmed, and my sister and I sat at her kitchen island, reminiscing about the week we had just shared.

"Sis, I can't even believe all you did this week. I could never thank you enough."

My sister, with the most sincere and loving expression, replied to me, as if it should have been obvious, "Kathy, I would do *anything* for you."

Shame overwhelmed me and I burst into tears. I covered my face with my hands and sobbed. I felt completely unworthy of such devotion.

You see, just three years prior, at age 57, my sister had undergone a double lung transplant. After suffering with pulmonary fibrosis for nine years, it had gotten to the point where she was on oxygen full time, and if new lungs weren't offered soon, she wasn't going to make it.

Finally, in January of 2019, the call came and new lungs were waiting for her. The feelings that surrounded the surgery were like a bowl of Halloween candy; sweet and happy, excited that my sister was getting a new chance at life, yet also sad and salty, knowing someone had to pass in order for this to be happening, and then dark and rich with concern that the surgery would take her life and not save it.

She obviously did survive the surgery, but she remained on a tracheostomy for three months, rendering her unable to speak. The image of walking into her room in the ICU unit and seeing her lying there on the bed still haunts me. She was barely recognizable as my sister. This was a tiny, frail version of the energetic dynamo I knew her as. Instantly, I felt a pit in my stomach. How was it that at age 49, I felt so ill equipped to handle this situation. I had absolutely no idea what to do, what to say, how to help her. I had never before felt so uncomfortable around my sister. I hated it. I was present, but I didn't feel like I was helpful or as caring as I wanted to be, but I just didn't know how.

But the shame that was breaking me at that moment was stemming from more than that. As a result of the lung transplant procedure and the subsequent recovery, it was discovered that my sister's kidneys had been damaged beyond repair, now requiring her to undergo dialysis three times a week and the need for a kidney transplant. I am completely embarrassed to say that when I heard this, my first thought was, *please don't ask me.* The truth was, the thought of removing one of my kidneys terrified me. Sitting with my sister in her kitchen that August evening held up a mirror to my selfishness and it filled me with tremendous guilt, knowing that if the table had been turned, there would have been no hesitation on her part to help me.

My sister had always known how to care for people. She would take it upon herself to do things that I would feel afraid to do because of the fear of being too intrusive. That fear of being nosey or overbearing has always been an easy excuse for me to do nothing.

It never occurred to me that even the smallest act of kindness can have such an impact on a person.

I have received hundreds, if not thousands, of texts, cards, and small gifts meant to inspire and support me, and each one of them has touched my heart in ways that I would not have expected. A sense of helplessness is a common sentiment I hear from many, but they don't realize what each and every thoughtful deed means to me. They inspire me to do better and be better if I'm given the chance to be healed.

Then there are the family members and friends who went way over and above what was expected of them. When Chris was called out of town for work, they showed up with their sleeves rolled up and ready to help, even if that meant physically lifting me onto the toilet or putting me in the shower. They cooked for me and did laundry. They not only took care of me, but they also walked and fed our dog Stephi. And in between all of that, we laughed and reminisced just like nothing was wrong. In those moments I got to be me again. I could forget my diagnosis for a little while and remember how enjoyable life could be.

But the most significant kindness I have had to endure is from my husband. This is where the "suffering the kindness of others" really resonates. I now rely on him for every meal, for getting me on the toilet, into the shower, getting dressed and getting in and out of bed. As a wife, this destroys me inside. It makes me feel more like a child than a wife. I still see him as the sexy man I married, but I can't help wonder how he sees me now. My once strong and limber body is morphing into something I barely recognize. If I do somehow make it through this, will he ever be able to see me as sexy again? Will he still be attracted to me?

Along with the burden of caring for me, he also has the burden of making up for my lost income, taking care of all the bills, the laundry, as well as shopping for and cooking all the meals. It's overwhelming at times. I know he often feels the weight of the world on his shoulders. How could he not? It's completely unfair to him. But he does it. And he does it with such love it brings tears to my eyes. It breaks my heart and causes me to mourn the life we had. What I wouldn't give to have one more slow dance in the kitchen or cuddle on the couch. At times, I am overcome with feelings of loneliness and I miss him so much.

When we said our vows before God, we declared each one sincerely. However, neither of us could have imagined that in just six years of marriage, the "in sickness and in health" component would already be put to the test. If not for our shared faith in God, I don't know how we would be surviving this. It seems when one of us begins to stumble and doubt, the other is there to lift up and encourage. There are still moments we cry together, struggling to understand the why, until we inevitably acknowledge that only God knows the why, and also the how and when the suffering will end, and we agree that we need to surrender it all to God, *again*. In the meantime, we are both trying to learn as much from this experience as we can.

I've had many people tell me that they are in awe of my positive attitude, my strength, and perseverance, but that's not me, that's nothing but the grace of God. And all of these incredible people that God has placed in my life fuel my faith and help me to keep going. They are heroes to me. They really are the ones to be in awe of.

Thank you, God, for continuing to teach me through this ordeal. Thank you for allowing me to suffer the kindness of others so that I may recognize others' suffering, so that I can reach out in the same love that you have shown me and the same love that you poured out onto me through my family and friends.

CHAPTER 14

Sharing Is Caring

Recently, Chris confided in me about his daughter's heartfelt apology for not being in touch more or visiting more, and she admitted to him that she was uncomfortable around me because she didn't know what to say or what to do. I applaud her for exposing what I and so many are afraid to. As much as I have tried to not allow this illness to define who I am, and I have made great efforts to just be me to help others feel more comfortable, there is no denying that this is a big part of my life right now. Especially since I can't walk anymore, and I spend my time either in bed or in a wheelchair.

These feelings are very reminiscent of when I became a widow. I could sense that people were uncomfortable around me and so I did my best to just pretend that everything was normal, I was still me. For the most part, I didn't mind doing that. In fact, it would allow me brief moments of respite from the heaviness of my reality. But if I'm being candid, sometimes I wanted people to ask me about it, ask me how I was doing, feeling. For a period of time, grief was a large part of my life, just like this illness is now. I'm happy to talk about it, answer your questions. Dying is a major life event, just the same as new life is. If someone had a baby, you wouldn't avoid the topic of their new baby. True, one is a truly joyous occasion and the other is heartbreaking, but both are important occurrences in one's life. To avoid either of those conversations would be an obvious and uncomfortable intention.

Sometimes I wonder how I will feel when/if I'm healed and I look back on this time. I have a feeling that it will be similar to how I feel when I look back to the time after Erik died. For a moment in time there was just life and death and survival. Nothing else really mattered or was important. All I had to think about was getting through the current day.

I will also look back and cherish my time with God, how close He feels, just like during my period of grief. I think of the shepherd that leaves the 99 for the one that is lost or hurt. When Erik died, I was the lost sheep. Now I'm the hurt sheep. In each instance, He has gathered me up and placed me in the safety of his arms. His love and mercy have cradled me.

Looking forward, however, I yearn to return to the herd of 99 again. In times of relative ease, God's presence may seem less pronounced, yet it remains a source of underlying peace. Surrounding ourselves with other believers allows us to minister to each other, to practice the love and mercy that Jesus teaches us. That's why fellowship is necessary. People are important. Love is crucial.

There have been times when I envied Erik's death, the suddenness of it, living his best life one minute, and the next he's in heaven eternally with Jesus. But if I step beyond my daily trials, my ever-increasing limitations, my frustrations, I have to admit that if I had to choose, I would choose this. This whole year of slowly progressing immobility and loss of function has been worth being able to experience this overwhelming love, and also to have the opportunity to share God with people, something I was always hesitant to do. I no longer feel afraid of offending people, turning people off from me. I feel confident

now that for however much time I have left, I will continue
to share God and His love and His mercy, and I will share it
with the joy that is only experienced by embracing a personal
relationship with God.

However, there is a moment of regret that haunts me.

A Moment of Regret

California 2006: *Where the heck am I going to eat? Are there
seriously no restaurants near this hotel?*

It was the first day of a multi-day arbitration that required
daily transcripts, meaning they wanted them before the next
morning. It's an incredible amount of work and I had no time
to waste commuting which necessitated staying in a hotel in
the outskirts of LA. It was already 6 p.m. so I needed to grab a
quick dinner and get back to the hotel to start working on the

The closest option that I found was a shopping mall. I
wouldn't normally pick a mall food court for dinner, but I
really needed to be quick. I parked and quickly walked into
the entrance of the mall. Sbarro pizza caught my eye. *Perfect.
A quick slice and I'll be out of here.* Happy to find that it wasn't
busy, I settled into a seat in their small establishment with my
slice of pizza and soda.

As I started to eat, I noticed a couple seats over an old
woman sitting by herself wearing an old cotton dress that she
could have borrowed from Edith Bunker. Her gray hair was
pulled up in a bun and her face looked gentle but weathered.
Perhaps she caught my eye because she didn't look like someone
who would frequent a shopping mall. Instead, she looked like
a grandmother who should have been standing over a pot of
homecooked chicken and dumplings. Further glances in her
direction revealed that she wasn't eating, just staring ahead of
her. But what struck me most was how sad she looked. *I should*

233

go see if she wants to join me. What? Where the heck did that come from? I didn't have time to sit and chat.

But she's hurting.

My heart felt so heavy for her and I felt this nudging that I needed to do something but I didn't know what. *God, I don't have time right now.* However, God just got more persistent and the urge kept getting stronger the more I looked at her. *I need to tell her that God loves her.*

Come on! I can't walk up to a complete stranger and tell her that God loves her! She'll think I'm nuts!

As I continued the battle in my head, the old woman gathered herself and left the tiny restaurant. *Sorry, God, she's leaving. Nothing I can do now.* I felt relief, thinking I was off the hook now, but I also felt deep regret, like I was letting God down.

Within just a few more minutes I finished my dinner and started to make my way out of the mall. I departed the food court and passed by stores and fought temptations to stop and shop a bit. I was almost to the doors of the mall that I entered through, and there she was, the old woman, sitting on a bench with the same sad stare. I instantly felt that pang in my heart again. It was as if I could feel her sadness. It was a mixture of heartbreak, sorrow, and loneliness.

I have to do something, but what?

I thought, what if I got her something. I looked around at the nearby stores. Banana Republic, no. The Gap, no. Kay's Jewelry, no. Spencer's Gifts, *hmmm, maybe.* I didn't have time to search the mall because I didn't know how long she would be sitting there.

I walked quickly into Spencer's and started to scan the items, but all I saw at first was the fart machines and silly trinkets. *Maybe this was a bad idea.* But then my eyes landed on some stuffed animals. They were small and inexpensive and

I thought, who doesn't like stuffed animals? I picked a soft brown teddy bear, paid for it, and tore off the tag as I left the store.

I was relieved to find the woman still sitting on the bench, yet I was also apprehensive about approaching her. How was I going to do this? My stomach was turning in knots. I had no doubt that God was adamant that I do this, but at the same time I was so uncomfortable doing it. *Kathy, come on. Just give it to her. What's the worst that can happen? You're being silly.*

I took a deep breath and marched right up to the woman and I bent down in front of her, right where her sad stare was focused. Before she could even acknowledge me, I shoved the bear in front of her and said, "You're supposed to have this."

And then I was gone. I didn't wait for a response and I don't even remember the look on her face. I turned around and walked quickly through the mall doors and to my car. It felt right that I had done something, but it has forever nagged me that I didn't do what God had originally called me to do. I should have reached out to her, been friendly, or at the very least I could have said "God wants you to know that He loves you" instead of "You're supposed to have this." I mean, jeez, I could have, at the very least, said, "*God* wants you to have this."

I still think about that woman and wonder what she was going through, what she had asked God for, with the hope that my gesture, as pitiful as it was, was enough of an answer to a prayer for her not to give up on God.

God, thank you for putting that woman in my path and forgive me for not doing all that you called me to do. I pray that if You ever trust me like that again, that I can share you openly and lovingly, without fear of judgment or rejection. Please, Lord, make me braver.

CHAPTER 15

God Hears Every Prayer

In the midst of suffering, it's easy to wonder if your seemingly countless prayers and pleas for mercy are being heard. We cry out to God in despair, begging for relief, for an answer, for a resolution, and wait expectantly for a response. When one is not received in what we feel is an appropriate amount of time, we feel defeated and disappointed.

Whenever I'm feeling disgruntled with God, I try to see things from His perspective, a practice I grudgingly admit that I learned from my mother. To simplify it, I imagine me as the child and He as the parent. As a child, I have limited understanding due to the mere fact that I haven't lived long enough to acquire the knowledge and foresight that my parents possess. As parents, their job is to love and protect, but that doesn't mean I'm precluded from experiencing pain or loss. In fact, there are instances where pain and discomfort are necessary, such as going to the dentist or getting a shot. A child may scream and cry because they don't understand the purpose of the pain, but it doesn't deter the parent from doing what is necessary to protect their future. Imagine all that parents do for their children that they have no knowledge of, such as researching the best schools, finding suitable baby-sitters, making sure bills are paid so that they have a home, heat, and water. Children have no concept of the magnitude of what is involved in caring for them. Similarly, we can't begin to fathom all of the things God does for us that we never see. After all, God's wisdom and timing are both limitless. In both instances we need to trust that our earthly parents and Heavenly Father love us and want only the best for us.

In my experience, the most important element of prayer is that it comes from our hearts. When we approach God with love and sincerity, the volume and frequency of the prayer are inconsequential.

Quiet Prayers

August 1993: I was 23 years old and I was living in New York. I was still a nanny and attending court reporting school at night. My mother, who had survived an aortic aneurysm once, had been diagnosed with another, which was very rare. This time, however, she refused the surgery that had saved her the first time. It had been a difficult surgery and a long recovery, and she just didn't have it in her to go through it again. I think she felt she had raised my sister, my brother, and me, and she was ready to go be with Brad again.

Diagnosed with the second aneurysm in 1992, the doctors didn't know for sure how long it would take to burst, whether it was weeks, months, or possibly years, but it would eventually take her life. We tried to talk her into having the surgery but her mind was set. My mother was at peace with the ticking time bomb that resided inside her.

I always had a practice of praying before falling asleep, a ritual that my mother taught me when I was a little girl. After mom's diagnosis, my first prayer every night was *Dear God, please don't let mom die.* Every. Single. Night.

In August of 1993, I attended the Emmaus retreat that changed my life. This was where I learned that God wants to have a relationship with us. That He wasn't just this far away presence sitting up in heaven looking down on us. He was actually *with* us, always, everywhere. I learned that our conversations aren't just one way, prayers going up, but that He communicated to us, too, if we were open and observant to what He wanted to tell us. This was comforting to me.

There was one topic, though, that made me a bit uneasy as soon as it was brought up. God's will. As it was discussed and clarified, I recognized right away that I had not been praying the prayer that I should have been. I began to understand that God's will was much more important than mine, what I wanted.

When I returned home from the weekend retreat, I got ready for bed and turned out the lights. As I laid my head on the pillow, my body filled with dread about what I knew I had to do.

With trepidation, I amended my nightly prayer. *Dear God, please don't let mom die.* And then I took a took breath and winced, like I expected it to hurt, and added as quickly as I could, maybe with the thought that if I prayed it really fast, God wouldn't hear it, and finished with *but Your will be done.*

There! I did it! I felt immediate relief doing what I knew I had to do, and I fell into a deep and wonderful sleep.

The next day I woke feeling…just normal actually. Nothing memorable. But that afternoon, after I had prayed that prayer the night before, my sister called me.

"Kathy, mom's in the hospital. It's the aneurysm. You need to come. We're not sure how long she has left. We're making arrangements to get you here."

My very first thoughts were, *I just killed my mother!* It was an awful, wretched feeling. Why, oh, why had I allowed God to take her? Why did I have to pray that prayer?

The next day I flew to Grand Forks and my father picked me up at the airport. As we were traveling from the airport to the hospital to see my mother before she died, my father was talking but I was only catching pieces of what he was saying. My heart was so heavy and my mind was trying to grasp that I was 23 years old and about to lose my mother.

"—woman named June."

"—been dating a while."

"—moving in."

I came out of my fog enough to finally put it together.

"Dad, are you getting married?"

Nonchalantly my dad responded, "Yeah. Why don't you come over tonight and you can meet her."

I looked at my dad and it was like I didn't recognize him. *Are you kidding me right now? You're bringing me to see my dying mom and you want me to meet your girlfriend?*

"No, Dad. I'm not meeting her tonight." Words I thought and finally had the courage to say. The rest of the drive was quiet.

As I walked into my mother's hospital room, she was awake and very alert. As soon as she saw me, a huge smile spread across her face. "Kathy! I'm so glad you're here! I told God I had to wait for you!" I went to her and embraced her, filled with so many mixed feelings. She was always so happy to see me. *Why?* I always felt angry at her. *Why couldn't I let it go? Why did everything about her irritate me so much, even now?*

Knowing that this moment in time would be etched in my memory for the rest of my life, I was determined to get it right. I prayed that I could be the daughter I wanted to be and I could love my mother for all of the wonderful things she did for me.

Please, God, help me to love my mom. Take these feelings of anger away and help me to forgive her.

For the rest of that week, my mother hung on and God granted me peace and love for her. He lifted that heavy burden of hurt and anger and helped me to remember how much she loved me and all she had done for me growing up. He brought to light that my dad was not the perfect man I thought he was, and my mom was not the contemptuous woman I accused her of. I started to see my parents through adult eyes, and I saw two people who had done the best they could.

During Mom's last days, she was in and out of consciousness, the morphine doing its job of making her comfortable. Periodically she would open her eyes and focus them on the corner of the room or above our heads and say, "Oh, look who's here," and she would name family members that had passed. At one point, while her eyes were still closed, she said, "Who's rubbing my feet?"

Sherry and I just looked at each other as we sat in our chairs on the side of her bed and shrugged our shoulders.

In case we had any doubt that Mom was ready to go, at one point she opened her eyes and looked up to the ceiling but she was clearly seeing beyond it. Excitement in her voice she said, "This is it! I'm going!"

I was sitting next to her, holding tightly to her hand, tears flowing, one notch before sobbing.

Mom turned her eyes to mine. "I see water in your eyes. Don't be sad! Be glad!" she exclaimed, and she closed her eyes. Within just a few seconds, her eyes popped open again and she looked around. Obviously disappointed with seeing us and not Jesus, she said, "Oh, damn! I'm still here!" It was hard not to laugh and it lightened the bereft mood in the room.

At 5 a.m. the next morning, the hospital called. Mom had peacefully gone to Jesus in her sleep. Despite the sorrow I felt for my loss, I was incredibly grateful that God had granted her prayer to wait for me.

Later that week I accepted my dad's invitation to meet his fiancée, June. She was actually a very pleasant woman, eerily similar to my mother in appearance and demeanor. That, along with some acquired maturity, allowed me to greet her cordially. I didn't stay long but I knew my dad appreciated the effort.

As I walked to my car, Dad followed alongside me. It was a beautiful August evening and the fireflies were beginning to let their presence be known, the kind of evening that made you forget about the long, harsh winters.

"So, when is the funeral going to be?" he inquired.

"Saturday at 10:00. Will you be going?"

"If you want me there, I'll be there," he said resolutely. "But you know there's going to be a lot of people who won't want to see me."

It was true. Many of my mother's family members and friends hadn't forgotten how my father left after 36 years of marriage, breaking my mother's heart. Ultimately her cause of death, if you ask some. To know that my dad would endure their resentment to be there for me filled me with a feeling I hadn't felt in quite a while, in fact since before my dad left us. Now I was his little girl again and he was putting my needs before his own. He was being a father. I had to admit it felt nice.

"You're my dad and I want you there," I said, allowing myself to be honest.

"Then, I'll be there."

He was correct in his prediction. There were plenty of glaring eyes and whispers, but my dad just took it in stride. And that was the day my father redeemed himself in my eyes. He was loving and consoling, just like the dad I remembered as a child. Instead of fixing a blister on my finger after my first bowling tournament, he was mending my broken heart.

It meant everything to me to have him there and to feel like I had a father again.

Thank you, God, for hearing my prayer and for waiting for me to be ready to give my mother back to you. Thank you also for restoring my relationship with my father, blessing both of us with your grace.

Frequent Prayers

Experiencing loss produces a relentless awareness that is difficult to ignore. As soon as I returned to St. Louis after losing Erik, the thought of saying goodbye to Kira began to haunt me. Questions nagged at me, like *how long do I have left with her? How will she die?* As often as the thoughts popped up, I prayed that she wouldn't suffer and that I would be there when she passed, however, I wanted her death to be from natural causes. I couldn't stand the thought of putting her down.

Six months after Erik passed, Kira required surgery on one of her knees to repair the cartilage that had been causing her pain. As the years progressed, so did the degeneration of the cartilage in her other knee. Though she would occasionally lose her stability and fall to her belly, she never cried. However, it was alarming to watch her struggle to get herself back up. The veterinarian prescribed a drug that would help with inflammation and pain but it was not meant to be taken long term, longer than a year to two years. She warned that it would eventually overcome her kidneys which would result in death. Now approaching 10 years old, I figured if this gave her a better quality of life for the next year or two, it was worth it. I couldn't have a 90-pound dog that couldn't walk.

Kira was our sensitive but fearless dog. Fireworks and thunderstorms didn't bother her a bit. But if Chris or I were in the kitchen and we started to raise our voices, not in an argument, but perhaps reciting an occurrence that bothered us that day, our voices indicating that we were frustrated or unhappy, no matter where Kira was laying, she would slowly and carefully, with effort, pick herself up and walk dutifully into the kitchen and sit at our legs, lean into them, and look up as if to say, "I'm sorry this happened. I'm here. Just go ahead and give me a pet and you'll feel better." And she was almost always right.

Akitas originate from Japan, and the first person to bring one to the United States was Helen Keller. It was a gift from the Japanese emperor. Though Akitas are treacherous hunters, they were also bred to watch over children while the parents worked in the fields. Kira demonstrated this twice, and each time I was amazed.

One instance was on the new deck that Erik had built at his brother's house. We were enjoying a Sunday barbeque to celebrate it, with several of Marshall's friends and their families. We had a number of children in attendance ranging in the ages from 1 to 9 playing on the deck, and several couples either sitting at the table or standing and leaning against the deck railing. James, the parent of the youngest guest at the party, sat on the deck as his 18-month-old scooted around on a little toddler ride-on.

Kira was laying at my feet and just surveying the goings-on of the deck. Suddenly she stood up and went and planted herself on the second step that led down to the lower level. Our friend's son had pushed himself right up to the ledge and none of us had noticed, but Kira did and she used her large body to block him. She didn't even look at the toddler. She just stood right in his way. James, the father, who had been hesitant about allowing Kira out with us and around the small kids, with a sheepish grin, said, "Okay, that's pretty cool."

The next time was several months later. Our friends Tim and Julia came for dinner one evening and they brought their little toddler, Niam. He wasn't walking yet, but he could crawl like the dickens. We all congregated in the kitchen as dinner was cooking, chatting and laughing. Kira was laying in her corner near the dining room table, out of the way and just observing. We had all been keenly aware of Niam as he crawled around, taking things out of his hand that he had found on the floor or directing him to alternative things to play with. Somehow a few minutes lapsed without any eyes on him, and he disappeared. We all ran into the living room. Not there. We ran to the stairs. Niam had crawled up two stairs, almost to the landing that then turned and continued to the second floor. And there was Kira, laying right on the landing, directly thwarting any idea that Niam had about exploring the second floor. Again, she paid no attention at all to the giggly little guy, she just did what came naturally to her. She protected.

Akitas are also known for their fearlessness and their keen hunting skills. This was demonstrated several times on walks throughout the years. Periodically, as we walked near yards covered with ivy, Kira would suddenly stop and stare intently into it. Her body remained completely still. Suddenly, with the prowess of a cat, she would fling her massive body 2 feet into the air and pounce on the ivy as she thrust her nose deep into it and pull out a mouse. Dutifully, when I said, "Drop it" she would spit it out, and the dazed little field mouse would run off to live another day. As I stood in awe, Kira was completely unimpressed with her catch.

Mice weren't the only prey that she hunted.

After Erik passed, Kira and I were spending much of our time in the large backyard, and I would see Kira act similarly, but there was no ivy. She would stare at the yard. At different times, it was different places. Occasionally she would pounce, take out some big piles of grass and dirt just by a couple of sweeps with her large and powerful paws, but nothing but dirt surfaced. Until one day. She had been honing her stares into a smaller area. Then she pounced hard, and this time after two or three big pawfulls of grass and dirt, she shoved her nose in the hole and pulled out a mole.

I had never in my life seen a mole, nor did I know that they lived underground like that. It was disgusting. Kira plopped herself on her belly, mole still in mouth, clearly proud of her catch and not nearly as willing to let his one go. "Drop it!" I commanded.

Kira's face: "Nope."

She let the mole fall from her mouth in between her front paws. Without moving her head, her suspicious eyes followed my every movement as I tried to get a better look at this thing.

Part of me felt bad because I knew how long she had hunted this menace. I wondered how much time she actually spent just contemplating her next moves and devising a plan to catch it. But I also didn't know what diseases they could possibly carry and I did not need a sick dog. I went into the house and retreated with one of her milk bones.

It was a tough choice for her at first but finally the bone won out. As she crunched away on the giant milk bone, I discarded the dead (thankfully) little yard rat to the dumpster.

By August of 2021, I could sense Kira was slowing down. She began eating less and her walking slowed tremendously. Little did I know, however, she had one more hunt in her.

Well, on this last week of her life, as we strolled slowly and I allowed her to sniff whatever she wanted for as long as she wanted, she once more stopped and stared at a yard next to the sidewalk. It had been quite some time since the previous mole trick and I wasn't expecting to see anything like that again. But much to my surprise, with the same powerful paws she removed enough dirt to pull out another mole. I was in shock. However, this time the older and wiser Kira didn't have a problem letting it go. I think she just wanted to feel the thrill of one more hunt.

Two nights later, I was scheduled to take an in-person asbestos deposition that was a day's drive away. That meant leaving the day before and staying the one night and possibly more. Most of my work was still remote due to COVID but by August of 2021, there were some cases being scheduled in person. This ate me up. I did not want to leave Kira in the state that she was in, but I also didn't want to let my office down. The days leading up to it, I prayed, *God, I'm so fearful of leaving Kira. Please, if her time is coming, let me be there. I will give this over to you and trust your will.*

Two hours before I would have to leave for the deposition, I received notice that it had been cancelled. *God, thank you so much. I just know that your hand was in this somehow.*

That night before bed, both Chris and I commented that Kira didn't seem herself. She seemed restless and a bit confused but eventually settled down in the hallway where she slept most nights.

At about 2 a.m., a noise stirred me. It wasn't loud but I had been keeping an ear open in case Kira needed something. I pushed the covers back carefully so as not to wake Chris and slid out of bed. As I entered the hallway, I could see that Kira was no longer laying in the spot where she had been. I quietly made my way down the staircase. By the time I got halfway down, I could see Kira on her belly, all four legs sort of splayed out. She was almost to her water bowl and it appeared that that had been her intended destination.

Once I got closer, I could see that she couldn't move. I knew better than to try to lift her up. That had been attempted multiple times through the years and it never worked, nor was it appreciated. If I just gave her enough time, she would find a

247

way to get herself up. Somehow I sensed this was different. Her breathing was heavy, her gums were white.

I went into the living room and got myself the warmest blanket I could find and wrapped it around me. I didn't plan on returning to bed any time soon. If this was Kira's time, I wasn't going to abandon her.

I got comfortable on the cold kitchen floor and curled up next to her. Kira lifted her head as I lay down in front of her. She didn't look confused anymore, but I saw something I had never seen in her eyes before. Fear. I looked into her eyes and I told her, "It's okay, Kira. It's okay. I'm here."

She closed her eyes and I rubbed her head, "You're a good girl, Kira." And for an hour or so we just lay there together. Occasionally she would open her eyes long enough for her to see that I was still with her and then close them again.

After a couple hours had passed, I wanted her to know that it was okay for her to go. I didn't know if dogs were like humans, who had the capability to hang on, but I told Kira, "It's okay. I'm going to be okay. I understand you have to go."

By this time the tears were rolling down my face in such quantity, I could barely see. Kira set her large head on the floor and she closed her eyes. Suddenly I felt another presence. It wasn't Chris. When it occurred to me who it was, the tears came even harder.

"Kira, it's okay. Erik is here for you. I promise, I'm going to be okay. You did a great job and I love you so much. I will never ever forget you."

Within minutes, her head lifted in an unusual manner and then rested back on the floor, and that was it, she was gone. I looked out in front me but I wasn't focusing on anything. "She's yours again, Erik," I managed to squeak out before grief once more overtook me. My heart broke all over again for a dog I hadn't wanted but was always meant to be mine.

God, thank you so much for making it possible for me to be here. You are so good and faithful, Lord.

I lay on the floor with her the rest of the night. I didn't wake Chris up. I wanted to be alone with her for the last time. I wanted to memorize the softness of her fur, the colors on her face, the freckles by her nose. I wanted to feel her closeness and appreciate all that she had been to me: My friend. My protector. My family.

When morning came, Chris came down the stairs and found me asleep with my hand on Kira. It appeared that Kira was sleeping as well, and so as I woke and explained what happened, he burst into his own sorrowful tears. She had become as much a part of his life as she was mine. When we were composed enough, Chris found an old sheet to wrap her in. Before closing it, he went to his garden and picked the most beautiful rose to place on top of her before he wrapped her up. It was such a touching gesture.

The following evening, as Chris hosted a business meeting at the house, I donned my ear buds and went for a walk. As I travelled all the same sidewalks that Kira and I had traversed, I could still feel her. I could see her sniffing all her favorite spots. As I entered the familiar park I often brought Kira to, I decided to sit on the park bench and just be, something I hadn't done in quite some time.

Again, the tears just poured out of me from overwhelming sadness. As I sat and let the tears fall, something occurred to me. The sadness that was taking over at this moment wasn't just the loss of Kira. It was the realization that in the not-too-distant future, Kira would be merely a memory. A deeply cherished memory for sure, but a memory, nonetheless. At that moment, on the bench in the park, I could still *feel* Kira. It was like she was just off sniffing a tree in the distance. But experience had taught me that that would change. There would soon come a day when it would be normal to open my eyes each morning and not see Kira's dancing eyes and wet nose just inches from my face, wishing me a good morning. When I would walk down the sidewalk and not see her trotting in front of me. And *that* thought broke my heart. But at the same time, I knew that it was supposed to be that way. That is the only way we move on and open up that space in our heart for what may come next. That is the moment I understood why some people had difficulty letting go of their grief. For as painful as grief is, the thought of not feeling our loved one around us any longer is an even greater pain.

God, thank you for hearing every single prayer, whether it's whispered one time late at night or shouted repeatedly in the midst of despair. You see every pain we suffer and every sadness we endure. I pray for patience, Lord, while I await your response, and acceptance when your answer doesn't correspond to my expectations or desires. Help me to always remember that Your ways are not mine, but that You are always good and know best.

Epilogue

And that is where I am going to leave you, with both of us still wondering, "Does she make it?"

You see, my story was never about my looming death, it was about the tragedies of life (we all have them) and overcoming them, learning from them, and not letting them define who we are. It's about the glory of suffering and finding God in the midst of it, trusting Him with all of our anguish and despair, and finding gratitude. Remembering that with gratitude comes trust; and with trust, peace; and with peace, patience. And if we are patient, and we trust God, our circumstances will change in ways we can't even imagine because God is God and He can do anything.

Acknowledgements

I would be completely remiss if I did not devote time and pages to the people who have helped me along this journey, and in doing so, teaching me how to be a more devoted spouse, loving sister, and caring friend.

To my friends Chandra, Tammy, Jody, Lori, Lorna, Glenda, and Dawn, for all the trips to come see me, the hours you spent traveling and away from your families and responsibilities, for all the laughs and glasses of wine enjoyed together, for making me feel like me again, for the meals cooked, the foot rubs, the stretching and massage, the prayers, the gifts, the cards, the texts, for long talks on the patio and giggles before bedtime, for your selfless eagerness to pitch in and be helpful wherever you could be, for offering things I could have never asked for, thank you.

To my friends Christy and Babs, for weekly Zoom happy hours that were both serious and silly, for the prayers and tears and laughs and kindness, for helping in ways that I would have never expected, thank you.

To my friends in St. Louis, old and new, especially Tami, Laurie, and Peter, thank you for every meal you brought over, for every evening spent reminiscing and enjoying our history together. Thank you for your cards, your care, your concern, and your prayers. Thank you for teaching me how much small kindnesses can mean to people who are struggling, regardless of how well you know them. It won't be forgotten.

Proverbs 27:9, "A sweet friendship refreshes the soul."

To all of my friends near and far, each of you has refreshed my soul. You have proven that true friendship knows no distance nor boundaries. I will be forever grateful for the time spent with each of you and I look forward to many more years of being your friend!

To Michael, my hair stylist, and Mary, my masseuse, for your incredible kindness and going over and above and doing more than I could have ever asked for. Your generosity and your loyalty fill my heart with gratitude.

To my family in Minnesota, for your unconditional love, for giving me a week I will never in my life forget, for your selfless generosity, for all the hugs and laughs and boat rides, for trips to visit me and texts to encourage me, you all amaze me with your kind and loving hearts.

To Haley and Tosha, who every day inspire me by example to be the best version of myself that I can be, to never stop learning and growing. I am in awe at the women you have become.

For all my other family spread out across the country, thank you for all your love, your concern, and keeping me in your thoughts and prayers. I appreciate each one of you and love you all so much.

To my sister, my person, my first call, my friend and my confidante, for your gracious hospitality and selfless generosity, our late-night talks and sunny deck coffee chats, for your homemade cinnamon rolls and hugs before bed, for being an inspiring example of defeating the odds and unwavering faith, and for always, always making me feel cherished and loved, I thank God every day for you.

To Dawn, my honorary sister, my best friend, for the daily texts of prayer and encouragement, for the guidance and love and empathy, for riding the roller coaster with me, front row, hand in hand. For every tear we've shed and laugh we've shared, your presence in my life for the past 30 years has largely influenced the person I am today. If not for you, I am not this version of me.

To Katy, Alyssa, and Poppy, simply stated, there is no book without you.

Thank you, Alyssa, for following through on your promise to God when God answered your prayer to help Poppy. Whether your brew was meant to save my life or just extend it, you can feel content that God's will was certainly done. Thank you for not only extending and possibly saving my life, but for your weekly check-ins that I always enjoyed. Thank you for the laughs we shared and all your helpful insights and explanations that we both know went right over my head much of the time. But mostly, thank you for your friendship.

Thank you, Katy, for listening to God and sharing my story and praying for me. We've never spoken other than via text, yet I treasure your friendship and I feel as though we are deeply connected. You inspire me with your perseverance and your tenacity and your willingness to do whatever it takes to be there for your family. I look forward to sharing a bottle of wine with you and toasting to our good health!

To my husband, Chris, I can barely find the words. When I met you, all of a sudden, my whole life made sense. At a time unknown to me, way before we met, God placed you in my heart so that I would recognize you when you came into my life. From our first cup of coffee at Starbucks, I had such a deep sense that I already *knew* you. I had no idea what lay ahead for me, but God picked the perfect person to travel this journey with. You will forever have my deepest and most sincere gratitude for every hug, kiss, and prayer, for all the meals prepared with love, the cups of coffee on the patio, for anticipating my needs before I could even voice them, for taking on way more than your share, for loving me with such devotion and reassurance. Every day my prayers of gratitude include you. You are my heart.

My Heavenly Father, who sees all and knows all, thank you for everything that you are teaching me, for all of your grace, such amazing grace. Thank you for showing me over and over again that You love me by all the amazing people you have placed in my life and that truly You can do anything, that no ask is ever too big for you.

To Jesus, thank you for the example of how to suffer, how to love and be patient, and how to find glory and purpose in my suffering.

And the Holy Spirit, thank you for your presence every single day, for your peace and your guidance. Truly, without you, I would be a dark empty shell, filled with doom and despair. You lift me up and help me to see beyond myself, the bigger picture, and it fills me with conviction that my suffering is a blessing for myself and also for others.

BE SURE TO LOOK FOR KATHY'S NEXT BOOK, "*THE YEAR AFTER I WAS TERMINAL.*" ENJOY THIS EXCERPT:

Preface

*I*n June of 2022 I was diagnosed with terminal cancer. I was told that my breast cancer had metastasized in the meninges, the thin layers that protect my brain and spinal cord, with no known cure and that I had less than a year to live. Throughout the year my body slowly and steadily became numb and weak to the point I could no longer walk.

Within a few months of my diagnosis, I came to terms with the fact that I most likely was going to die. I forbade myself to believe that death was a certainty because only our Father in Heaven knows our expiration date, but I had to concede that it didn't look good.

However, if life has taught me nothing, I knew that no ask was too big for God if we hand it over to Him. In June of 2023, that belief was confirmed and celebrated when we received the news that the cancer in my spine was gone, therefore canceling my terminal status.

I wish I could say that was the end of my story. When I was initially diagnosed with terminal cancer, I held the belief that I would either be healed in Heaven or here on Earth. I didn't foresee a third option.

But God threw me curve ball.

MEET THE AUTHOR, RESERVE YOUR COPY
OF KATHY'S UPCOMING BOOK, AND JOIN
OUR COMMUNITY OF CANCER WARRIORS

GO HERE: KATHYHEEB.COM

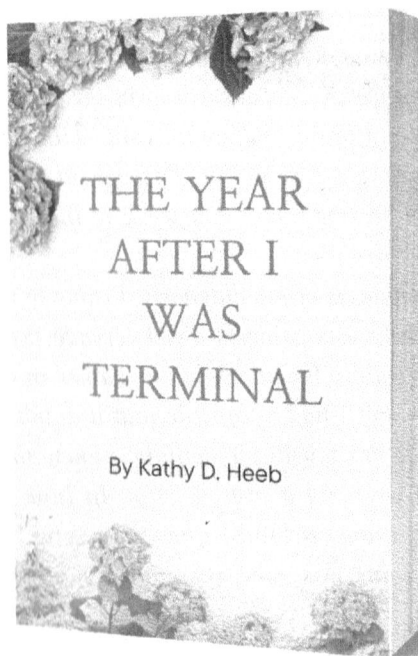

THE YEAR
AFTER I
WAS
TERMINAL

By Kathy D. Heeb